The LDS Family Travel Guide

Sharon, Palmyra and Kirtland

ALSO AVAILABLE

The LDS Family Travel Guide – Independence, Nauvoo and Winter Quarters
The LDS Children's Activity Book – Independence to Nauvoo

The LDS Family Travel Guide

Sharon, Palmyra and Kirtland

Becky Cardon Smith

LDS Family Travels, LC

Published by
LDS Family Travels, LC
Orem, Utah
www.ldsfamilytravel.com

All photographs by Greg and Becky Smith except where noted:
* Courtesy LDS Church Archives (LDSCA)
° Courtesy, Community of Christ Archives, Independence, Missouri.

First Printing:	March 2003
Second Printing	March 2005
Third Printing	May 2005
Fourth Printing	March 2006
Fifth Printing	March 2007
Sixth Printing	March 2008
Seventh Printing	July 2009

Layout by Shane Allman Art & Design

ISBN: 978-0-9720782-2-1

TABLE OF CONTENTS

PENNSYLVANIA AND NEW YORK

OHIO

Acknowledgements

The only thing more difficult than writing a first book is writing a second. Without the positive support from family and friends before and after the publication of *Independence, Nauvoo, and Winter Quarters*, I never would have attempted another travel guide. As with the first volume, my thanks begin with my parents, Louis and Robin Cardon. They are to blame for the travel bug that I've been bitten by for most of my life. They were also indispensable during the lengthy editing process. Greg, my husband and companion in all of life's travels, has been unfailingly enthusiastic in his support for this and all my projects. In addition, each of my children has made his or her distinct contribution. Melissa's editing skills and writing advice were much appreciated. Shane's assistance with the maps and wry sense of humor helped me immensely. Erik's positive outlook and enthusiasm for life are contagious. Michelle's radiant smile and well-chosen words of encouragement were always welcome bits of relief.

In addition to family, I would also like to acknowledge and thank the LDS visitors' center directors and local historians whose input and insights were essential to my research.

As I learn more about Church history and the early Saints, I am ever more impressed and inspired by their faith and diligence. They are truly co-authors of this book.

Chapter One
Successful Traveling

Traveling to Church historical sites is fun and informative; it can also leave a positive and lasting impact on you and your family. Think of the wonderful opportunity you have to discuss the importance of baptism, next to the Susquehanna River where John the Baptist appeared to Joseph and Oliver. Read the Prophet's account of the First Vision as you sit with your family in the Sacred Grove. Relive in your imagination Joseph's painful experience of being beaten, tarred and feathered as you stand in the room in which a sleeping Joseph lay by his infant child before being dragged away by an angry mob. Learn about the many spiritual events that occurred in Kirtland as you walk through the Newel K. Whitney store, visit the Isaac Morley farm and tour the Kirtland Temple. Everyone will enjoy a visit to the beach near what was once an important Lake Erie port used by arriving Saints and departing missionaries.

Those who have used our other guidebook will know the importance of advanced preparation to ensure a successful travel experience. Just as building a home without a set of plans is unwise, a trip without advance thought and discussion is also on shaky footings. I can't promise you that even a well planned trip will be entirely free of problems and an occasional "near-catastrophe." (We have come to count on a few of these laughable memories.) I can promise you a more productive, informative, and less stressful traveling experience if you follow the **"3 Ps."**

PLANNING
PREPARATION
POSITIVE TRAVEL ATTITUDE

PLANNING

Just as I would never take a trip with a tour guide who hadn't announced an itinerary and a price, I would never leave on a family trip without doing some advanced planning on what to see and how much time and money to spend. While I am not suggesting you make an itinerary that leaves little room for spontaneity, I have found that the more thought and planning we do before we leave, the more I can relax and enjoy the trip. The time spent answering the following questions will result in better informed decisions now and fewer unpleasant surprises later:

How many days do we need for this trip?

Though it is possible to cover all of the places mentioned in this book on one trip, many of you will probably be visiting only some of the listed sites. If time is short, it is usually better to focus on one or two areas rather than hurrying to many places for a brief visit. Allow yourself at least eight full days if you plan to visit all of the areas covered in this book. In describing the various Church history stops, we have also indicated some of our recommended "must see" sites and suggested lengths of stay. But before you make any travel arrangements, read through all the chapters for more detailed information on the sites and talk to others who have been there to learn from their experiences. In planning your trip, allow an extra cushion of time for unexpected delays or stops. It would be frustrating to spend the time and money getting to the sites and then leave feeling that you had missed something important. Several local guides and LDS visitors' center directors have commented, "I wish people could know beforehand what we have here and about how much time they need. It is sad when visitors come up to us and say 'we only have a few hours, what should we see?'"

The following is a suggested travel and time itinerary; see the corresponding chapters for further information.

- **Sharon, Vermont** – The closest airports for those planning to fly into this area include Burlington, Vermont (1.5 hour drive), Manchester, New Hampshire (1.5 hour drive), and Boston, Massachusetts (2.5 hour drive). Others have flown into New York City, Washington D.C., or Philadelphia, etc., to see the sites in those areas before driving to Sharon. If you are in the Boston area, consider the one-hour detour through Topsfield. I suggest you plan one full day in the Sharon area to spend some time at the Joseph Smith Memorial, see the store where Joseph Sr. met Lucy in Tunbridge, visit the site where Joseph had his leg surgery in West Lebanon, and drive by the home rented by the Smith family while living in Norwich. All of these sites are in close proximity. If time allows, visit a nearby farm for a maple syrup demonstration, stop at the granite quarry in Barre, or take a scenic drive through one of the quaint New England villages.

- **Whitingham, Vermont** – This small village is the birthplace of Brigham Young and is a nice rest stop when driving south from Sharon before continuing on to South Bainbridge, New York and Harmony, Pennsylvania. Allow 30 minutes to visit the monument to Brigham Young and his birth site. The distance from Sharon to Whitingham is about 100 miles (about a two hour drive).

- **South Bainbridge, New York** – Now called Afton, the town was known as South Bainbridge at the time Joseph and Emma came here to be married. If time is short, take 5 minutes to exit the freeway and see the historic marker. But we suggest you allow 30 minutes to drive by the Josiah Stowell home and several other sites before continuing on. The distance from Whitingham to Afton is roughly 175 miles (four hour drive). However, en route to Afton, you will pass by Cooperstown, the home of the National Baseball Hall of Fame (607-547-0200). For those who love soccer, consider stopping at the National Soccer Hall of Fame (607-432-3351) located in nearby Oneonta. Your children may vote to make Cooperstown an afternoon stop and lodging spot. For more information, or to receive a free tourism packet, contact the Cooperstown Chamber of Commerce at 607-547-9983. The closest airport for the Cooperstown area is either Albany or Syracuse.

- **Harmony, Pennsylvania** – Now called Oakland, this area is a brief but important stop. Allow 30-60 minutes to view the site of Joseph and Emma's cabin, the site of Emma's childhood home, the cemetery where Joseph and Emma's first child and several extended family members are buried, the Monument to the Aaronic Priesthood, and the beautiful Susquehanna River. The distance from Afton to Oakland is about 25 miles (a 45 minute drive on a country road).

- **Fayette, New York** – Many significant and spiritual events took place at the Peter Whitmer farm in Fayette. Allow 1 hour or more to tour the visitors' center and the reconstructed Whitmer home. The distance from Oakland to Fayette is about 110 miles (about a 2 1/2 hour drive). The suggested route is part interstate and part country roads.

- **Palmyra, New York** – The closest airport to Palmyra is Rochester (24 miles away), but other airport options include Syracuse (67 miles away), Buffalo, and Albany. Allow two full days to visit the many "must see" sites in this area, including the Hill Cumorah and its visitors' center, the Sacred Grove, the Smith family log cabin, the Smith frame home, the Book of Mormon Historic Publication Site, the Palmyra Temple, and the Martin Harris home site. There are also many "nice to see" sites, including the Erie Canal, Swift Cemetery, and more. The distance from Fayette to Palmyra is about 37 miles (a 45 minute drive). The distance from Palmyra to Kirtland is about 260 miles (about a 5 hour drive).

- **Mendon, New York** – Many are unaware that several important Church historical homes and sites are located very close to Palmyra in the town of Mendon. Allow one hour to drive by the homes of John Young (Brigham Young's father), the site of Brigham Young's home and mill, the Tomlinson Inn, Solomon Kimball's home, and to visit the Tomlinson Corners Cemetery where Brigham's first wife, Miriam Young, and many members of Heber C. Kimball's family are buried. Mendon is located about 20 miles (a 30 minute drive) southwest of Palmyra.

- **Niagara Falls, New York** – A trip to Niagara Falls can be a day trip from Palmyra, a detour while driving to Kirtland, or a flight into Buffalo followed by a short drive. The distance from Palmyra to Niagara is about 100 miles (a 90 minute drive). Depending on your schedule, allow several hours or up to a full day and night. You don't have to be a newlywed to enjoy the beautiful views and misting activities on both the American and Canadian sides.

Read the corresponding chapter for detailed information. Be sure to note the specific identifications needed for traveling to the Canadian side.

- **Kirtland, Ohio** – The closest airport for this area is Cleveland (45 minute drive). We suggest you allow two days to see the many significant sites in this area. (To see it all in one day is a very rushed experience.) Especially exciting are the five sites that have been completed or restored by the Church and dedicated in May 2003. "Must see" sites include the LDS visitors' center and the walking tour of Historic Kirtland which includes the schoolhouse, sawmill, ashery, Whitney Store, Whitney home and Johnson Inn. Other "must see" sites are the Morley farm, the Kirtland Temple, and the John Johnson farm in nearby Hiram. "Nice to see" sites include the North Kirtland Cemetery, quarry, and Fairport Harbor. If time allows, there are a variety of other activities to enjoy including a hands-on nature center for children, amusement parks and more. The distance from Palmyra to Kirtland is about 260 miles (about a 5 hour drive) while the distance from Niagara Falls to Kirtland is about 200 miles.

While driving on New York State Thruways, you will notice service centers or deluxe rest stops. We have stopped at several of these centers and find them great rest stops. They usually include a gas station, information center often manned by informative individuals, free maps, restrooms, small gift shops, and usually at least two fast food dining choices (McDonald's, Burger King, Wendy's, etc).

How should we travel?

Time, expense, and family needs should all be considered when making this decision. Consider flying if time is short and your destination far. The closest airports to the sites covered in this book have already been listed. On one trip, we flew into Boston and rented a car. We spent eight days traveling to all of the sites mentioned in this guidebook and our total driving mileage was about 1,600 miles. We then flew from Cleveland to St. Louis, rented another car, and drove up to Nauvoo.

You may have family members to see or business to conduct in a certain area and may want to combine this with a visit to some of the nearby Church sites. If you are thinking of flying, watching for good airfares and being flexible as to which airport you use will usually result in a good rate. Before booking your flight, decide your starting and ending points and consider all your options. We rarely fly in and out of the same airport when traveling.

Driving is an option for those with a more flexible time schedule and for those who want to visit family or see other places en route to the Church sites. Driving may also be more economical than flying, depending on the number in your group. Remember to factor in the price of gas, food, and lodging in deciding which option is best for you.

Another transportation choice is traveling by train. For further information, check with your local Amtrak center, call 800-872-7245, or check online at www.amtrak.com.

Where should we stay?

As with travel options, you will usually have many choices in lodging within a varied price range. Listed at the end of the chapters are some of your lodging choices. In the smaller towns, we have listed almost all of the lodgings available. In larger towns, we have listed those we have either stayed in, inspected, or have had recommended to us. The difficulty in recommending lodging and Bed & Breakfast (B&B) choices is that we all have different expectations in cost, location, and sleeping accommodations. As a rule of thumb, in deciding whether or not to list a place, we ask ourselves, "Is it clean?" and "Would we stay here for that price?" We have also included RV and camping sites. Many of the lodging choices and RV sites in the smaller towns fill quickly in the summer and we suggest that you make reservations ahead of time, especially when traveling with a family.

How much will it cost?

The cost of your trip will depend on you and your preferences. We have tried to list a wide variety of lodging and dining choices. We have also included information on grocery stores, discount variety stores, souvenirs, and shopping buys. Though it would be hard to calculate your trip expenses down to the dollar, you can set a flexible budget in advance by adding up your lodging expenses, gas, admission fees, and factoring in food and souvenirs. Be sure to add a NOMB (not on my budget) amount.

You will notice that some of the lodgings, restaurants, gift stores, and admission-charging sites have a **D** identification next to their description. This denotes a 10% discount given by the business to those who show this travel guide. (There are a few businesses providing other discount options; read the corresponding chapter for additional discount information.) We have tried to be as accurate as possible on admission fees and other pricing information. Realizing that prices and circumstances change, we strongly suggest you verify prices and discounts before making your purchase or reservation. **As you call to make lodging reservations, please mention you have this guidebook and request the discount.**

Our hope is that the discounts you receive will more than offset the cost of this book. We all like a bargain!

What should we see and do?

All family members have their own personality, likes and dislikes. Read through the chapters and highlight the things that interest you and your family. Make a list of the "must see or do" and "nice to see or do" sites and activities that interest you. Talk to others who have been there and see what they enjoyed most. As a family, discuss what you most want to see and do. Many of the areas offer both Church sites and recreation options; try to incorporate some of both in your trip. Family compromises are easier to make and less emotional when largely worked out at home.

In helping you decide which sites to see, we have given some historical as well as other helpful information. While this is not a history book, it is easier to appreciate and remember what you are seeing when you know some of the background information. Our hope is that we have given you enough information to help you grasp the importance of each site or incident and have left you with a desire to know more. There are many other informative Church history books that go into more detail than we have. Our book is a success if we inspire you to see the sites, make them more meaningful for you, and whet your appetite with a desire to learn more.

Put pencil to paper.

Now the real planning begins. Though I am not suggesting you make an hour-by-hour schedule, I find things run more smoothly on our trips if we have a basic outline already planned. Included at the end of this chapter are daily schedule forms. Use one for each day of your trip. Write in where you will be in the morning and pencil in the "must see" and "nice to see" sites and activities that you and your family have chosen. We make sure we see all the "musts" first and the "nice to sees" if we have time. Some of your daily schedules may include sites in several towns as you travel that day. At the bottom of the page, fill out your lodging information. I find it is more convenient to have all of my important information on one sheet of paper and in a set place. You may want to copy your daily schedule forms and leave them with those who need to know your whereabouts in an emergency. The expense section is provided for those who want to keep a record of daily expenditures.

Please don't feel after reading this far in the book that planning your trip is going to be a lot of work. I promise you that the planning process is really quite easy and painless. You will find that it will actually get you excited and looking forward to your trip. Filling out the daily schedule sheets will only take a few minutes, but you will refer to them often while traveling. You will find that all of the advance planning is well worth the effort and will allow you to relax and enjoy the trip.

You will also notice that there are blank pages at the end of each chapter. Use them during your trip to write down feelings or thoughts you have, amusing things that are sure to happen, facts you've learned, names or numbers you don't want to forget, or other information you want to remember. Hopefully, this book will serve not only as a guidebook but will also be a record of your wonderful trip!

PREPARATION

This is the second step to a successful trip. Once you have made the basic planning decisions, you can focus on preparation. Understanding beforehand more about the sites you will be seeing helps to enhance the learning experience. There are several suggested videos that could be shown at family home evening either before your trip, or as a review after your return. All of the following videos (except the last one) are available through Church Distribution or Deseret Book. (They may also be available to check out from your local ward library.)

- *Church History* – This DVD set is a "must have" for all families. For the minimal cost of $6, you can add this wonderful collection to your family library. The first disc covers the beginnings of the Church in New York, 1805-1831. Included on this disc are: Overview of Church History, The First Vision, The Three Witnesses, Organization of the Church and much more. The second disc covers Kirtland to Nauvoo, 1831 – 1846. Included on this disc are: I Remember Kirtland, Zion's Camp, Joseph Smith: The Man, Remembering Nauvoo, and more. The third disc covers the trek west in 1846 to the present day. Included on this disc are: A Legacy more Precious than Gold, Faith in Every Footstep: The Epic Pioneer Journey, Windows of Heaven and more.

- *A Voice From the Dust* – Included on this video are: How Rare A Possession: The Book of Mormon (includes story of Parley P. Pratt), A Marvelous Work Begins (dramatization of major events leading up to the Book of Mormon), The Three Witnesses (the lives and testimonies of these three men are portrayed), and For Us! (the importance of the Book of Mormon).

- *Moments From Church History* – The video includes: The First Vision (perfect for those visiting Palmyra), Restoration of the Priesthood (actually filmed in Harmony), The Windows of Heaven (Lorenzo Snow and the revelation on tithing), Joseph Smith: The Man.

- *Doctrine and Covenants and Church History* – Included on this video are: The First Vision (previously mentioned), Restoration of the Priesthood (previously mentioned), Organization of the Church (filmed at Whitmer home with President Kimball), Parley P. Pratt Finds the Book of Mormon (President Benson discusses the importance of Book of Mormon and previously mentioned video), Windows of Heaven (previously discussed), Revelation of Priesthood (President Hinckley talks about the events surrounding the restoration of the Priesthood).

- *Teachings from the Doctrine and Covenants and Church History* – This video includes: A Search for the Truth (Wilford Woodruff's search for the true Church), The Works and Designs of God (Martin Harris recounts the lost manuscript experience), A Man Without Eloquence (conversion story of Brigham Young), Zion's Camp (events from Zion's Camp), The Heart and a Willing Mind (Heber C. Kimball and his mission to England), Joseph Smith: The Prophet of the Restoration (review of the Prophet's life).

- ***Fourth Witness: The Mary Whitmer Story*** – A wonderful story to view before visiting Fayette.

The **Gospel Art Picture Kit** has many pictures of pioneer events and early Church leaders (also available through Church Distribution and may be available to check out in ward libraries). The historical summaries on the back are brief and concise and make for great discussions.

Reading through the chapters in this book and discussing some of the stories, sites and events will heighten your awareness and appreciation of what you will be seeing. Discussing ahead of time sections from the Doctrine and Covenants that were received at the various locations you will be visiting can also be helpful. In addition to the reading preparation, there are several things we suggest you include in your packing. Though the secret is to travel light, the following may come in handy:

- **Scriptures** – You will find moments when you will want to sit at the sites and read from them. If this is your first time seeing these sites, consider recording the date of your visit next to the applicable D&C section heading. Years later, you will be reminded of your trip as you read about a revelation given at Harmony, Kirtland, etc.

- **Additional resources such as articles, books, or suggested readings** – Bring a few select books or copy specific pages or stories to be read at the sites. (For example while at West Lebanon, read the story of Joseph's leg operation as written by his mother.)

- **Church Hymnal** – A travel size hymnal is available through the Church Distribution. Being able to sing selected hymns at specific sites is a memorable experience. We suggest several hymns but you will probably think of many others.

- **Free tourism packets** – Many of the local chambers of commerce offer free tourism packets that include maps, brochures, and other helpful information. Call the numbers listed in this book at least a month ahead of your trip to ensure the packets' arrival before your departure.

- **Family records with names, birth dates, or burial sites** – Check before leaving to see if you have any relatives who once lived in the areas you will be visiting. If so, you may want to visit the local town recorder's office to copy genealogical information, locate burial sites, or take pictures of specific churches, buildings, etc. for your records.

- **Maps of your driving route** – We have found it very helpful to purchase a map covering our driving route. You may also want to print more detailed driving instructions using mapquest.com, mappoint.msn.com, or randmcnally.com.

- **A roll of quarters** – Some of the roads and sections of the interstates are toll roads. We have found it very handy to have ready change.

- **National Parks Pass, AAA Card or AARP Card** – This pass may come in handy for those planning to use park camps/RV sites. Some of the sites or restaurants may offer discounts to AAA or AARP members.

- **Granola bars, dried fruit, and other snack items** – I have found it especially helpful to carry snacks for younger children. Our mealtimes may vary but their hunger pains are fairly constant.

- **Basic first aid supplies** in compact container, prescription medicine, antibacterial **wipes**, and travel-size **tissues** (sometimes needed in restrooms).

- **Good walking shoes, backpack** or fanny pack to carry water, **umbrella, snacks,** etc. Check the Internet before leaving to see the weather forecast for your travel area.

- **Sunglasses, sunscreen, bug repellent, and camera.** I also recommend you always have **water** on hand as the areas covered in this book have high heat and humidity in the summer.

- **Travel games, crayons, coloring books,** etc. for entertaining younger children while on the road.

POSITIVE TRAVEL ATTITUDE

This is the third requirement for a successful family travel experience. Simply put, this means "go with the flow." Traveling is exciting but it isn't always just what you expected. You may get hot, become tired, sleep in a bed not as comfortable as your own, or walk a few more miles than you are accustomed to. Your meal may not be as good as mom's, or you may have to stand in a long line. My advice is to put it into perspective, laugh it off, and deal with it. You and your family have a great opportunity that many others would love to have. To learn about Church history at the sites, to get the special feeling that comes from being on sacred ground and to catch a glimpse of what our pioneer ancestors went through is an incredible experience. It is worth putting up with a few inconveniences. Make the most of your trip and ignore the minor things. All too soon you will be back home wishing you could revisit those special places. If everyone in your group travels with this PTA, you will laugh more, whine less, appreciate more, criticize less and return home with a heart full of memories, a mind filled with facts, and a suitcase crammed with well used clothes. Have a great trip!

Date: _____ Town: _____
Must See or Do:

_____

_____

_____

_____

_____

_____

Nice to See or Do:

_____

_____

_____

_____

Expenses:

_____

_____

_____

Lodging: _____
Address: _____
Phone: _____ Rate/Cost: _____
Misc/Notes: _____

_____

Date: _____ Town: _____

Must See or Do:

_____

_____

_____

_____

_____

_____

Nice to See or Do:

_____

_____

_____

_____

Expenses:

_____

_____

_____

Lodging: _____

Address: _____

Phone: _____ Rate/Cost: _____

Misc/Notes:_____

_____

Date: _____ Town: _____

Must See or Do:

_____

_____

_____

_____

_____

_____

Nice to See or Do:

_____

_____

_____

_____

Expenses:

_____

_____

_____

Lodging: _____

Address: _____

Phone: _____ Rate/Cost: _____

Misc/Notes: _____

_____

Date: _____ Town: _____

Must See or Do:

_____

_____

_____

_____

_____

_____

Nice to See or Do:

_____

_____

_____

_____

Expenses:

_____

_____

_____

Lodging: _____

Address: _____

Phone: _____ Rate/Cost: _____

Misc/Notes:_____

_____

Date: _____ Town: _____

Must See or Do:

_____

_____

_____

_____

_____

_____

Nice to See or Do:

_____

_____

_____

_____

Expenses:

_____

_____

_____

Lodging: _____

Address: _____

Phone: _____ Rate/Cost: _____

Misc/Notes: _____

_____

Date: _____ Town: _____

Must See or Do:

_____

_____

_____

_____

_____

_____

Nice to See or Do:

_____

_____

_____

_____

Expenses:

_____

_____

_____

Lodging: _____

Address: _____

Phone: _____ Rate/Cost: _____

Misc/Notes:_____

_____

Date: _____ Town: _____

Must See or Do:

_____

_____

_____

_____

_____

_____

Nice to See or Do:

_____

_____

_____

_____

Expenses:

_____

_____

_____

Lodging: _____

Address: _____

Phone: _____ Rate/Cost: _____

Misc/Notes: _____

_____

Date: _____ Town: _____

Must See or Do:

_____

_____

_____

_____

_____

_____

Nice to See or Do:

_____

_____

_____

_____

Expenses:

_____

_____

_____

Lodging: _____

Address: _____

Phone: _____ Rate/Cost: _____

Misc/Notes: _____

_____

Date: _____ Town: _____

Must See or Do:

_____

_____

_____

_____

_____

_____

Nice to See or Do:

_____

_____

_____

_____

Expenses:

_____

_____

_____

Lodging: _____

Address: _____

Phone: _____ Rate/Cost: _____

Misc/Notes: _____

_____

Date: _____ Town: _____

Must See or Do:

_____

_____

_____

_____

_____

_____

Nice to See or Do:

_____

_____

_____

_____

Expenses:

_____

_____

_____

Lodging: _____

Address: _____

Phone: _____ Rate/Cost: _____

Misc/Notes:_____

_____

Date: _____ Town: _____

Must See or Do:

_____

_____

_____

_____

_____

_____

Nice to See or Do:

_____

_____

_____

_____

Expenses:

_____

_____

_____

Lodging: _____

Address: _____

Phone: _____ Rate/Cost: _____

Misc/Notes:_____

_____

Notes

_____

_____

_____

_____

_____

_____

_____

_____

_____

_____

_____

_____

_____

_____

_____

_____

_____

Notes

Chapter Two
Church History Overview

To better appreciate and more fully understand the significance of the sites you will be visiting, it is helpful to have an understanding of what transpired within the area of Sharon, Vermont to Kirtland, Ohio. Though it is impossible to cover in detail the many significant events that occurred here, it is our hope that this chapter will help put many of these places, events, and people into an understandable sequence. Being more aware of what transpired at the sites you visit will increase your appreciation for the personal sacrifices made by the early Saints. These early members who embraced the gospel leave us a legacy of faith, love, tolerance, obedience, and commitment.

This abbreviated history begins with the blessings and hardships experienced by the Joseph Smith Sr. family in and around Sharon, Vermont. It continues with the family's move to Palmyra, New York and the miraculous events that transpired in the Sacred Grove and at the Hill Cumorah, followed by the official organization of the Church in Fayette, New York. This summary ends after yet another move – this time to Ohio. In Kirtland, the Saints first gathered as an organized entity and built the first latter-day temple, then were forced to leave it all behind in their exodus to Missouri. Further details about many of these events are given in following chapters of this book.

Tradition says that Lucy Mack first met her future husband, Joseph Smith Sr., while working at her brother's general store in Tunbridge, Vermont. On January 24, 1796, twenty-year-old Lucy married twenty-four year old Joseph Sr. The very generous $1,000 wedding gift from Lucy's brother and his business partner would be sorely needed just a few years later. The young couple spent the first six years of their marriage and had the first four of their eleven children while living on the Tunbridge farm.

In 1802, the young Smith family made the first of what would be many moves to nearby areas as they tried to make a living. After renting out their farm, the family moved to Randolph where they opened a mercantile store. But a business associate's dishonesty led to the failure of the business and

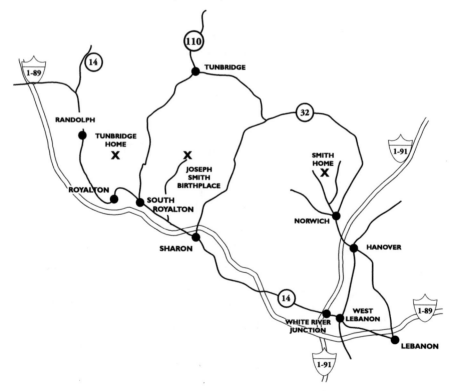

subsequent debts. Joseph Sr. and Lucy were able to pay what they owed by selling the Tunbridge farm and using their wedding money. In 1804, the debt-free but financially struggling family moved first to Royalton and then to a farm owned by Lucy's father in nearby Sharon, Vermont.

For the next three years, Joseph Sr. taught school during the winter and farmed during the summer, while living in the Solomon Mack farmhouse. The birth of their fifth child, Joseph Smith Jr., on December 23, 1805, was not only a blessing to the family but also a gift to the world. His birth fulfilled the prophecy by Joseph who was sold into Egypt that from his lineage would come another Joseph who would bring salvation unto the people.

From Sharon, the family moved back to Tunbridge about the time another son, Samuel, was born. In 1809, the family relocated to Royalton. During this second stay, Lucy gave birth to two more sons, though one lived for only 11 days. Joseph Sr. also had the first of what would be several profound dreams.

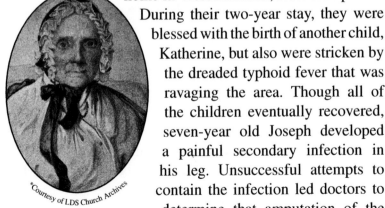

Courtesy of LDS Church Archives

Lucy Mack Smith

In 1811, the Smith family rented a home in West Lebanon, New Hampshire. During their two-year stay, they were blessed with the birth of another child, Katherine, but also were stricken by the dreaded typhoid fever that was ravaging the area. Though all of the children eventually recovered, seven-year old Joseph developed a painful secondary infection in his leg. Unsuccessful attempts to contain the infection led doctors to determine that amputation of the leg was necessary. But Lucy pled for yet another attempt to save the leg and so a complicated and rarely performed surgery was attempted. It was truly a miracle that the surgeon who pioneered the medical procedure was located in nearby Hanover, at the Dartmouth Medical School. The surgery itself was extremely painful, and Joseph endured it without taking any alcohol to deaden his senses, only asking that his father hold him in his arms. The surgery was a success; Joseph had a painful and slow but full recovery.

The Smith family moved in 1813 to a rented farm in nearby Norwich, Vermont. Here they were blessed with the birth of Don Carlos, but their financial situation continued to worsen. Two consecutive years of crop failure were followed by the "year without a summer" in which almost everyone's crops froze, including the Smith's. For Joseph Sr., this was enough. In 1816, he left to investigate an area where wheat was said to grow in abundance. He soon sent word back and arrangements were made for Lucy and their eight children to join him. Their destination and new beginning would be at Palmyra, New York.

The Smith family worked hard in their new home. They first lived in the Village of Palmyra, and by 1818 the family had saved enough money to make a down payment on 100 acres of wooded land in Manchester (two miles south of Palmyra). Joseph Jr. worked alongside his family clearing the land, planting seeds, and harvesting the crops. Though there was little time for formal schooling, Joseph took time to ponder spiritual matters, partly due to the unusual excitement over religion in the area. While feeling confused and wondering which church he should join, the young boy read James 1:5. This Bible passage provided both a challenge and a promise and Joseph became convinced that the answers he wanted would only come through prayer.

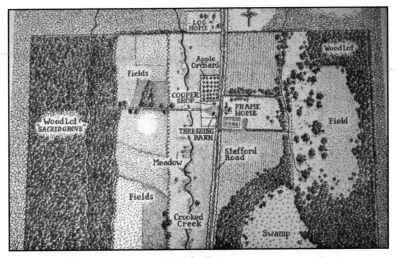

Smith Farm

On a beautiful spring day in 1820, fourteen-year-old Joseph went into the woods near the family's log home and knelt in prayer. He was almost immediately overcome by a thick darkness, which seemed as though it would destroy him. Calling upon God for help, Joseph saw a pillar of light over his head which descended until the light rested upon him and freed him from the binding darkness. Joseph saw two Personages standing above him in the air. He recorded the following: "One of them spake unto me, calling me by name and said, pointing to the other – *This is My Beloved Son. Hear Him!*" (JS–H 1:6-17). Joseph asked the Personages which of the churches he should join and was told that he must join none of them. Joseph was also told many more things which were not recorded.

Joseph F. Smith (sixth President of the Church) referred to Joseph Smith's experience, known as the First Vision, as "The greatest event that has ever occurred in the world, since the resurrection of the Son of God" (CHFT p. 36). Joseph had

Courtesy of Community of Christ

Joseph Smith

seen and talked with God the Father and his Son, Jesus Christ. Though Joseph would endure great persecution for the rest of his life, his personal testimony and account of the First Vision was something he would never deny.

Three years after receiving the First Vision, seventeen-year-old Joseph retired to his room late one Sunday evening on September 21, 1823. While he was earnestly praying and asking for further direction, the room suddenly filled with light and a heavenly messenger appeared. He was dressed in white and said he was Moroni, a prophet who had once lived on the earth. Moroni told Joseph about a record written upon gold plates that was buried in the nearby Hill Cumorah. Joseph was further told that the plates contained the fullness of the everlasting Gospel and that he was to translate these ancient records. Moroni's message was so important that he appeared two more times to Joseph that same night, repeating the message and adding additional information. The next day, as Joseph was coming back from the fields, Moroni appeared yet a fourth time. Later that same day, Joseph went to the Hill Cumorah as Moroni had instructed. He immediately recognized the spot where the plates were hidden, under a thick and rounded stone. After prying the stone away, Joseph saw the plates, the Urim and Thummim, and the breastplate in a covered stone box; but he was not allowed to take them. The angel Moroni instructed Joseph to return to this same spot on the same date every year to receive instructions and training.

Joseph's family never doubted the truth of his account of this experience and they were fully supportive of the great work he was called to do. The family of Joseph Sr. and Lucy had now grown to include nine children with the birth of a daughter in 1821 (two children had died in infancy). Their oldest son, Alvin, was skilled in building and had begun construction of a new frame home for the family. Tragically, just two months after young Joseph first saw the gold plates, his beloved older brother Alvin passed away on November 19, 1823. For the next two years, Hyrum took over the responsibility of completing the frame home until the family moved into it in 1825. During those same two years, Joseph returned to the Hill Cumorah and visited with the angel Moroni each September 22nd to receive further instructions.

To help with the family finances, Joseph and his brothers worked for others in addition to their work on the family farm. In October of 1825, Joseph and his father were hired by Josiah Stowell who lived in South Bainbridge, New York. While reluctantly agreeing to help Josiah look for a Spanish silver mine, Joseph boarded with the Isaac Hale family in Harmony, Pennsylvania. During his month stay at the Hale home, Joseph became acquainted with Isaac's daughter Emma. Joseph later worked for Josiah Stowell on his farm, and also for Joseph Knight Sr., another nearby farmer. Mr. Knight even loaned Joseph his horse and sleigh so that he could visit Emma in Harmony. Isaac Hale did not approve of Joseph's interest in his daughter. He considered Joseph uneducated and of dubious character. Because of Isaac's disapproval, Emma

Courtesy of Community of Christ

Emma Smith

and Joseph eloped and were married in South Bainbridge on January 18, 1827. The newlyweds returned to Palmyra to live with the Smith family in the frame home. Emma was warmly received by her new extended family; this was the beginning of a close relationship between Lucy and Emma.

Since his first visit with the angel Moroni, Joseph had gone through four years of preparation and training. On the evening of September 22, 1827, Joseph and Emma went to the Hill Cumorah. While Emma waited with the wagon, Joseph was allowed to take the sacred plates. Moroni also gave Joseph a charge: "that I should be responsible for them; that if I should let them go carelessly, or through any neglect of mine, I should be cut off; but that if I would use all my endeavors to preserve them, until he, the messenger, should call for them, they should be protected" (JS–H 1:59).

Joseph's desire to keep the plates safe was challenged almost immediately. Though his family and friends were supportive of Joseph and his work in translating the plates, others sought to steal them. The plates were hidden at various times in a variety of places including a hollow log, a wooden box, under a brick hearthstone, and in the loft of their cooper's shed. In December of 1827, unable to peacefully work on the translation, Joseph and Emma hid the plates in a barrel of beans in the back of their wagon and went to live with Emma's parents in Harmony, Pennsylvania. The young couple lived briefly with Emma's family and then purchased a nearby two-story home by the Susquehanna River from Emma's brother.

Joseph began translating the plates and was soon joined by Martin Harris in February of 1828. A farmer by trade, Martin received a spiritual witness about this important work. He came to Harmony knowing that Joseph was a Prophet and wanting to assist in any way possible. Martin went to

New York to show some of the translated
characters to three professors. He
also acted as scribe while Joseph
translated the writings on the plates
with the help of the Urim and
Thummim. However Martin's wife,
Lucy, was critical of the work and
felt that Joseph was an impostor.
Martin asked Joseph if he could take
the first 116 pages now translated
back to his home in Palmyra to show
the validity of their work. Upon asking
the Lord for permission, Joseph was
told "no," but in answer to Martin's

Courtesy of LDS Church Archives

Martin Harris

pleading, inquired again. After Joseph's third inquiry, Martin
was allowed to take the manuscript, with the promise that it
would only be shown to a few selected individuals. These
pages were subsequently stolen and Joseph's grief at their
loss was almost inconsolable. Another sad event was the
death of Joseph and Emma's first child, a son, who was born
and died on June 15, 1828.

For a brief time, Joseph was not permitted by the Lord to
continue the translation. But in the fall of 1828, Joseph was
again allowed to translate, with Emma acting as scribe. (He
was instructed not to retranslate the stolen portion.) The Lord's
promised assistant for Joseph was also being prepared. Oliver
Cowdery was a young schoolteacher who heard about the
young Prophet while boarding with the Smith family in their
frame home (see D&C 5:34, HC 1:32). In response to personal
prayer, Oliver felt that he should go with Samuel Smith to
visit Joseph in the spring of 1829. En route, they stopped in
Fayette to visit Oliver's friend David Whitmer. After Oliver
promised that he would write David about his impressions of

Courtesy of LDS Church Archives

Oliver Cowdery

Joseph, Samuel and Oliver continued to Harmony, arriving on Sunday, April 5th. Just two days after their arrival, Oliver began acting as scribe while Joseph translated.

For the next few months, Joseph and Oliver worked "with little cessation." Joseph was able to translate faster than ever before, completing over 500 pages. For Oliver, "These were days never to be forgotten ..." (JS–H 1:71, footnote). With little time for anything but translating, Joseph soon found himself almost destitute, with little food or writing materials. However, Joseph Knight Sr., upon learning of their needs, came from Colesville with provisions of food, lined paper, and money.

While Joseph and Oliver were translating, they became impressed with the importance of baptism and wondered how they could also have this blessing (see 3 Nephi 11:23-27). On May 15, 1829, Joseph and Oliver went into the woods along the Susquehanna River to pray concerning this desire. As they were praying, "a messenger from heaven descended in a cloud of light" (JS–H 1:68). The angel was John the Baptist, acting under the direction of the ancient apostles Peter, James, and John. He laid his hands upon the heads of Joseph and Oliver, conferring the Aaronic Priesthood (D&C 13:1). John the Baptist also promised that they would receive the Melchizedek Priesthood in due time. Joseph was then told to baptize Oliver, and Oliver in turn baptized Joseph. Though the exact date is not recorded, Joseph and Oliver also shortly thereafter received the Melchizedek Priesthood, which was conferred upon them by Peter, James, and John (D&C 128:20).

Susquehanna River

As promised, Oliver wrote David Whitmer soon after arriving in Harmony and testified of the truthfulness of the work they were doing. As persecution began to escalate in Harmony against Joseph, Oliver again wrote David, inquiring whether they might stay with the Whitmer family in Fayette, New York. David's response was to invite Oliver and Joseph to come and stay. David Whitmer first met the Prophet upon going to Harmony to bring Joseph and Oliver back to his family home; a close friendship was soon forged between Joseph and David.

During June of 1829, Joseph continued the translation of the plates in Fayette. The Whitmers were very supportive of Joseph's work, enabling him to finish the translation within the next month. During this same period, the gospel was taught in the area and was accepted by a number of people, including members of the Whitmer family.

*Courtesy of LDS Church Archives

David Whitmer

In the course of translating, Joseph learned that special witnesses would be chosen to see the plates and testify of their existence. Joseph received the revelation that Oliver Cowdery, David Whitmer, and Martin Harris could indeed see the plates and other sacred items (D&C 17:1-4). This came to pass when Joseph and these three men retired to a secluded spot behind the Whitmer home in June of 1829. Just a few days later, eight additional men were allowed to see and touch the plates in the privacy of the grove of trees near the Smith log home in Manchester. The written testimonies of these eleven witnesses are printed in the front of the Book of Mormon.

Following the completion of the translation, Joseph was anxious to have the Book of Mormon published. In August of 1829, arrangements were made in Palmyra with Egbert B. Grandin to print 5,000 copies of the book for a price of $3,000. To ensure payment, Martin Harris signed a mortgage agreement with Grandin. The printing of five thousand books was a large order for such a small local printing company, but a recent acquisition of a "Smith Press" enabled the work to go faster

E.B. Grandin

than usual. While Joseph returned to Harmony with Emma, Hyrum Smith and Oliver Cowdery supervised the printing process. On March 26, 1830, the first copies of the Book of Mormon were completed.

As directed by revelation, the Church of Jesus Christ was officially organized in the Whitmer home on April 6, 1830. Just ten years earlier, fourteen-year-old Joseph had experienced the First Vision in a grove of trees near his family's log home. Now in Fayette, in another log home, about 50 people gathered to witness this special event. The meeting began with prayer, a vote for official organization was taken, the sacrament was administered, and Joseph spoke and bore his testimony. The Prophet also received a revelation during this meeting as recorded in D&C 21. It was also a time of personal joy for Joseph as several persons were baptized that day including his father, Martin Harris, and Porter Rockwell.

With the first printing of the Book of Mormon completed and the Church officially organized, the spreading of the Gospel began in earnest. The Prophet visited with his friends in Colesville, New York, sharing his testimony and teaching. On June 28, 1830, thirteen people were baptized including Emma, Joseph Knight, and his wife Polly. Joseph's younger brother, Samuel Smith, presented a copy of the new scriptures to Phineas Young at the Tomlinson Inn in Mendon, New York. From this initial contact with the Young family, John Young and all ten of his living children and their spouses were baptized, including the

Courtesy of LDS Church Archives

Brigham Young

future prophet Brigham Young. Joseph Sr. accompanied by his son, Don Carlos, visited his parents, siblings, and extended family members who were now living in St. Lawrence County, New York. From this early missionary work, three generations of Smiths heard the gospel and were later baptized, including George A. Smith, who eventually became one of the Twelve Apostles. His grandson, George Albert Smith, would become the eighth President of the Church in 1945.

Courtesy of LDS Church Archives

Parley P. Pratt

About two months after its organization, the first general conference of the Church was held in the Whitmer home on June 9, 1830. A second conference was held three months later, September 26-28. With persecution increasing in Harmony, Joseph and Emma had recently returned to live with the Whitmer family. During this conference, Joseph commented that "the utmost harmony prevailed" (HC 1:18). About this same time, the Lord called Oliver Cowdery to "go unto the Lamanites and preach my gospel unto them" with Peter Whitmer, Parley P. Pratt, and Ziba Peterson also called to go with him (D&C 28:8, D&C 32:1-4). The missionaries taught the gospel as they went. They had great success in the area of Kirtland, Ohio, where they baptized 127 people.

The third and final conference in Fayette was held on January 2, 1831. During this conference, the Prophet received the revelation containing a second call for the Saints to "go to the Ohio" (D&C 38:32). While the Church was growing in the Kirtland area, the Saints in New York were facing increased persecution. At great personal sacrifice, the early Saints were obedient to the call to relocate to Ohio. Early that spring about 68 members from Colesville, 80 members from Fayette, and 50 members from the Palmyra-Manchester area headed west.

On a wintry day in February of 1831, Joseph and Emma (who was six-months pregnant with twins) arrived by sleigh at Kirtland, Ohio. Stopping at the Newel K. Whitney Store, Joseph jumped from the sleigh and entering the store exclaimed, "Newel K. Whitney! Thou art the man!" Surprised at this greeting, Newel put out his hand but was perplexed as to who this individual was. Joseph responded, "I am Joseph, the Prophet ... You've prayed me here; now what do you want of me?"(HC 1:146). The Prophet explained that he had previously had a vision in which he saw Brother and Sister Whitney praying for him to come to Kirtland.

Courtesy of LDS Church Archives

Newel K. Whitney

With the arrival of the Prophet, Kirtland became the headquarters of the Church with about 300 members living in the general area. That number soon increased as the Saints from New York began to arrive. Over the next seven years, from 1831 to 1838, Church membership in this area grew to over 2,000. The Kirtland era was an important period in Church history. It was a season of great spiritual outpouring, with many significant revelations received. It was also a period of many "firsts" which included: the first latter-day temple constructed, the welfare system first implemented, the first hymnal compiled, the first printing of the Book of Commandments, and the first educational program of the Church.

When Joseph received the commandment to build a temple, the Saints were struggling financially. Despite their personal hardships, they united in the cause of building the House of God. The first cornerstone was laid in July of 1833 and work progressed quickly as the men worked to provide stone from the quarry and prepared lumber at the mill. The women sewed clothing for the workers and even crushed their glassware to add sparkle to the exterior façade. On March 27, 1836, an estimated 1,000 Saints witnessed the dedication of the Kirtland Temple. W. W. Phelps had written a special song for this occasion, "The Spirit of God." Those in attendance were filled with inexpressible joy and many witnessed the outpouring of the Spirit. One week later, the Savior appeared to Joseph Smith and Oliver Cowdery in the temple and told them, "I have accepted this house, and my name shall be here" (D&C 110:7).

Kirtland was not only the headquarters of the Church, it was also the hub of missionary work. Fairport Harbor, located along the nearby shore of Lake Erie, became an important port for arriving

Kirtland Temple

Saints and departing missionaries. The missionaries left to preach the gospel amidst concerns over their families left behind and often with little purse or scrip. George A. Smith was so destitute that Joseph and Hyrum gave him scriptures and fabric for clothing, while Brigham Young gave him a pair of shoes. In another instance, the Prophet gave the coat off his back to a departing missionary. Joseph himself went on fourteen missions during his stay in Kirtland. In 1835, all of the Twelve Apostles were called on a mission to the eastern states (HC 2:222). Two years later, Heber C. Kimball and Orson Hyde left for England. Heber was so anxious to begin teaching the gospel that he leaped from the boat as it neared the shore at Liverpool. At great personal sacrifice, these early missionaries brought the gospel message to many future leaders and stalwart pioneers, both in surrounding areas and on foreign shores.

※ For Emma Smith, the Kirtland era was a season of great joy and of personal growth that came through adversity and sorrow. Emma had already moved seven times in the first four years of marriage. Upon their arrival in Ohio in January of 1831, she and Joseph spent the first few weeks at the Newel K. Whitney home before moving to the Isaac Morley farm. In April, Emma gave

Courtesy of LDS Church Archives

Heber C. Kimball

birth to twins, Thaddeus and Louisa, who died just three hours later. Soon after, Joseph and Emma received and adopted the nine-day old Murdock twins, whose mother had died while giving birth. While staying at the farm, Joseph worked on the inspired revision of the Bible, received many revelations and conducted the fourth general conference of the Church. During one of the sessions, Joseph and others witnessed many heavenly manifestations. The Smith family lived here for over six months before moving to nearby Hiram to live with the John Johnson family.

Joseph, Emma, and their newly adopted twins lived at the Johnson farm from September 1831 to September 1832. Many sacred and spiritual events occurred during their stay in Hiram. The Prophet and Sidney Rigdon continued to work on the inspired revision of the Bible, sometimes inquiring of the Lord about specific doctrinal questions. Several conferences were also held at the Johnson home. During these meetings, the publication of the Book of Commandments was approved and many important revelations were received. But in March of 1832, a tragic event occurred in which Joseph was dragged

Courtesy of LDS Church Archives

Sidney Rigdon

from his bed and then beaten, tarred and feathered by a mob. One of the twins, Joseph Murdock Smith, had been sick and died a few days later due to exposure to the cold night air during the mob's attack. Joseph and Emma had now suffered the death of the fourth of their first five children.

Joseph, Emma, and daughter Julia soon returned to Kirtland and lived for the next eighteen months in an apartment located in the Whitney Store. In November 1832, Emma gave birth to a son, Joseph III. The Prophet ran the affairs of the Church in an upstairs office and another room housed the School of the Prophets. On several occasions, Joseph and others experienced profound spiritual manifestations. The Prophet also received many revelations including a prophecy of the American Civil War (D&C 87), the Word of Wisdom (D&C 89), and the organization of the First Presidency (D&C 90).

In February of 1834, Joseph and his young family moved into a white-framed home just north of the temple. This was their final residence in Kirtland before their move to Far West, Missouri in January of 1838. While this was the family home, Joseph also conducted Church business, entertained many guests and visitors, and received several revelations here. It is likely that the seventh child of Joseph and Emma, Frederick G. Williams Smith, was born in this home.

Church membership was not only growing in Kirtland, but also in the Independence, Missouri area. After the introduction of the gospel in Missouri by Oliver Cowdery and the four other missionaries in 1831, the Prophet had received a revelation during a visit to Independence that this was "Zion," a place appointed and consecrated for the Saints to gather and build a temple (D&C 57). Church membership quickly increased with the arrival of the Saints from Colesville. After leaving their homes in New York, this group stopped briefly in Kirtland before continuing on to Jackson County, Missouri. While the Prophet, the Quorum of the Twelve Apostles, and many members lived in Kirtland, Church membership in the Independence area quickly grew to about 1,200 within two years. For the next few years, significant events were happening in both Ohio and Missouri, with leaders of the Church often traveling between the two areas.

As the number of Saints grew in Independence, so did the displeasure of some of the local citizens. Increased tension was followed by ransacking of homes and attacks on outlying settlements. Experiencing acts of violence and threats against their lives, the Saints were driven from their homes during the winter months of 1833. On February 24, 1834, Joseph received a revelation in Kirtland to organize Zion's Camp to help the Saints who had been driven from their homes (D&C 103). Though eventually disbanded by additional revelation, Zion's Camp proved to be a "refiner's fire" for future Church leaders. The Saints in Missouri first settled in Clay County before creating a new community in Caldwell County. By the spring of 1838, close to 5,000 members resided in and around Far West.

While Church members were temporarily enjoying peace in Far West, the Saints in Kirtland were experiencing increased persecution from without and apostasy from within. Fueled by the collapse of the Kirtland Safety Society, bitterness of former members and physical threats of violence made it unsafe for the Prophet to remain in Kirtland any longer. On January 12, 1838, Joseph was forced to flee from his home for safety. Emma (who was expecting a child) and the children joined him a few days later after which they made the long and difficult journey to Far West. Fearing for their own safety, most of the Saints in Kirtland also began to leave within the next few months and by the end of 1838, few active members of the Church remained in Ohio. Their vacant homes, abandoned possessions, and the magnificent Kirtland Temple remained as tangible reminders of an era that began with faith, commitment, and personal sacrifice.

Far West, Missouri had now become the headquarters of the Church. All too soon, the newly arriving Ohio Saints would be forced out of Missouri with the rest of the Church members. They would relocate in a swampy area at a bend of the Mississippi River and build a new city of faith and beauty – Nauvoo.

Our hope is that this overview has helped you put some of the important places, people, and events of this complex historical puzzle into place. We also hope it has whetted your appetite to learn more. There are many excellent books and articles regarding this early period in Church history. We encourage you to read on ...

- *Our Heritage*, published by The Church of Jesus Christ of Latter-day Saints.

- *Church History In The Fullness Of Times*, (Religion 341-43), published by The Church of Jesus Christ of Latter-day Saints. (Listed as **"CHFT"** after quotes given in this book.)

- *History of The Church*, by Joseph Smith (listed as **"HC"** after quotes given in this book).

- *The Revised and Enhanced History of Joseph Smith By His Mother*, edited by Scot Facer Proctor and Maurine Jensen Proctor (listed as **"HJS"** after quotes given in this book).

- *A Comprehensive History of the Church of Jesus Christ of Latter-day Saints*, by B. H. Roberts (listed as **"CHC"** after quotes given in this book.)

- *Joseph Smith - Rough Stone Rolling*, by Richard Lyman Bushman

- *Joseph Smith and the Restoration*, by Ivan J. Barrett

- *The Heavens Resound*, by Milton V. Backman, Jr.

- *Investigating the Book of Mormon Witnesses*, by Richard Lloyd Anderson

- *Joseph Smith's Kirtland*, by Karl Ricks Anderson.

Suggested articles in the Ensign include:

- *Ensign*, August 2001, "From New York To Utah: Seven Church Headquarters," p. 52.

- *Ensign*, May 1999, "The Witness: Martin Harris," p. 35.

- *Ensign*, October 2002, "Remembering Hiram Ohio," p. 32.

- *Ensign*, December 2001, "The Unfolding Restoration of Temple Work," p. 34.

(See previous chapter for list of suggested videos.)

CHILDREN OF JOSEPH SR. AND LUCY MACK SMITH

1. Son: Died at birth in 1796 in Tunbridge, Vermont.

2. Alvin: Born February 11, 1798 in Tunbridge, Vermont. Died November 19, 1823 in Palmyra.

3. Hyrum: Born February 9, 1800 in Tunbridge, Vermont. Died June 27, 1844 in Carthage, Illinois.

4. Sophronia: Born May 17, 1803 in Tunbridge, Vermont. Died August 28, 1876 in Colchester, Illinois.

5. Joseph Jr.: Born December 23, 1805 in Sharon, Vermont. Died June 27, 1844 in Carthage, Illinois.

6. Samuel Harrison: Born March 13, 1808 in Tunbridge, Vermont. Died July 30, 1844 in Nauvoo.

7. Ephraim: Born March 13, 1810 in Royalton, Vermont. Died March 24, 1810 in Royalton, Vermont.

8. William: Born March 13, 1811 in Royalton, Vermont. Died November 13, 1893 in Iowa.

9. Katherine: Born July 28, 1812 in West Lebanon, New Hampshire. Died February 1, 1900 in Ramus, Illinois.

10. Don Carlos: Born March 25, 1816 in Norwich, Vermont. Died August 7, 1841 in Nauvoo, Illinois.

11. Lucy: Born July 18, 1821 in Palmyra, New York. Died December 9, 1882 in Colchester, Illinois.

CHILDREN OF JOSEPH JR. AND EMMA SMITH

1. Alvin: Born June 15, 1828 in Harmony, Pennsylvania and died the same day.

2. Louisa: Born April 30, 1831 in Kirtland, Ohio and died the same day.

3. Thaddeus: Born April 30, 1831 in Kirtland, Ohio and died the same day.

4. Joseph: Adopted son born April 30, 1831 in Kirtland, Ohio. Died March 29, 1832 in Hiram, Ohio.

5. Julia: Adopted daughter born April 30, 1831 in Kirtland, Ohio. Died in 1880 in Nauvoo, Illinois.

6. Joseph Smith III: Born November 6, 1832 in Kirtland, Ohio. Died December 10, 1914 in Independence, Missouri.

7. Frederick Granger Williams: Born June 20, 1836 in Kirtland, Ohio. Died April 13, 1862 in Nauvoo, Illinois.

8. Alexander Hale: Born June 2, 1838 in Far West, Missouri. Died August 12, 1909 in Nauvoo, Illinois.

9. Don Carlos: Born June 13, 1840 in Nauvoo, Illinois. Died August 15, 1841 in Nauvoo, Illinois.

10. Son: Stillborn December 26, 1842 in Nauvoo, Illinois.

11. David Hyrum: Born November 17, 1844 in Nauvoo, Illinois. Died August 29, 1904 in Elgin, Illinois

Notes

_____

_____

_____

_____

_____

_____

_____

_____

_____

_____

_____

_____

_____

_____

_____

_____

_____

_____

Notes

Notes

Notes

_____

_____

_____

_____

_____

_____

_____

_____

_____

_____

_____

_____

_____

_____

_____

_____

_____

_____

_____

_____

Notes

_____

_____

_____

_____

_____

_____

_____

_____

_____

_____

_____

_____

_____

_____

_____

_____

_____

_____

_____

_____

Notes

_____

_____

_____

_____

_____

_____

_____

_____

_____

_____

_____

_____

_____

_____

_____

_____

_____

_____

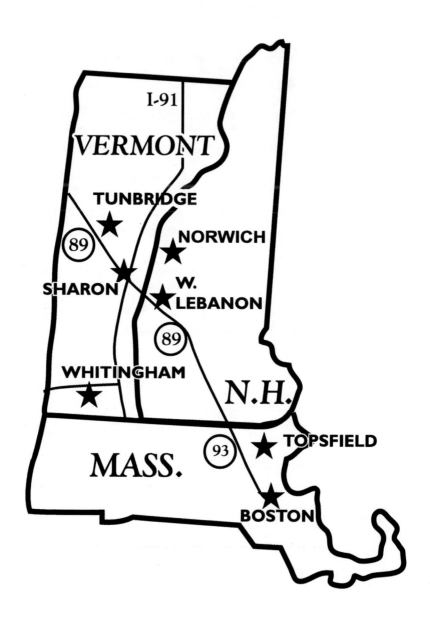

New England

Chapter Three
Topsfield

Topsfield, Massachusetts, with a current population around 5,800, lies about 20 miles north of Boston between Salem and Ipswich. Not far from the Atlantic Ocean, this New England area is steeped in early American history. Ipswich earned the title "Birthplace of American Independence," after strongly opposing British tax policies with the cry, "No taxation without representation!" Nearby Salem, once considered an important seaport, was also the birthplace of Nathaniel Hawthorne and the site of the infamous "witchcraft trials." For those of the LDS faith, the Topsfield area is important because it is the ancestral home of 5 generations of Smiths, including the Prophet's father Joseph Smith Sr.

PLANNING YOUR TIME

If you are going to be in the Boston area, consider taking a quick visit to Topsfield. Time spent driving through the commons, visiting the cemetery and seeing the Smith farmhouse site is about 30 minutes. Allow an hour if you are coming from the airport, stopping at the sites, and getting back on the Interstate (sometimes longer if Boston traffic is heavy). While this is not a suggested lodging stop, you will find several restaurant choices while driving on US 1.

GETTING THERE

Coming from the Boston airport, drive north on Route 1A. Merge onto US-1 N for about 8 miles, and take I-95 N for about 4 miles before taking US-1 N. (Topsfield exit).

SIGNIFICANT EVENTS

In 1638, fourteen-year old Robert Smith moved from Boston, England to Boston, Massachusetts. After his marriage to Mary French, Robert bought a farm in the Topsfield Township and had ten children. (The general location of this farm is west of the commons near I-95.) A son, Samuel, married Rebecca Curtis and also bought a farm in Topsfield. They had nine children, their first son being Samuel Smith Jr. He also married, had 5 children, and lived in Topsfield.

While living at what is now referred to as the Smith farm site, Samuel Jr. and his wife Priscilla had a son, Asael, on March 7, 1744. Asael Smith married Mary Duty and served as a soldier in the Revolutionary War. The couple would eventually have eleven children. Their second son, Joseph (Sr.), was born at the Smith farm on July 12, 1771. In 1791, Asael and his large family moved to Ipswich for about 6 months. They then moved to Tunbridge, Vermont where their son Joseph Sr. later met his future bride Lucy Mack.

Concerning Asael Smith, the Prophet Joseph Smith recorded, "My grandfather, Asael Smith, long ago predicted that there would be a prophet raised up in his family" (HC 2:443). After Asael had read the Book of Mormon, Joseph further stated that Asael "declared that I was the very Prophet that he had long known would come in his family" (HC 2:443). He was first shown the Book of Mormon when his son Joseph Sr. and grandson Don Carlos visited family members who were now living in St. Lawrence County, New York. Asael accepted the gospel but was too weak to be baptized. He died just a few months after his son's visit on October 30, 1830. His widow, Mary, traveled to Kirtland in 1836 to visit her extended family. She had also accepted the gospel and planned to have the Prophet baptize her. Unfortunately, she passed away at the age of 93, just ten days after her arrival.

SITES TO SEE

- **Commons** – After passing the Topsfield fair grounds on US-1, continue for half a mile and turn left at the signal onto High Street. Continue another half mile and you will reach a stop sign with the commons in front of you. Notice the large white Congregational Church located here. Some of the Prophet's ancestors were baptized at this site including Asael and Joseph Smith Sr. The existing building was constructed in the 1840s and is not the original church.

- **Marker Behind Congregational Church** – At the stop sign, continue on High Street which passes the white Congregational Church. The marker will be on your right, behind the church.

Marker Behind the Congregational Church

Erected by the Mormon Historic Sites Foundation and the Topsfield Historical Society in 2005, the marker tells of the significance of this area to the Smith family.

- **Marker at Smith Farmhouse Site** – This was once the home site of Samuel, Samuel Jr., and the birth site of Asael Smith and Joseph Smith Sr. Though the original home is no longer standing, the Smith well still exists in the backyard of this home. To see the marker at the farm site after leaving the Congregational Church, make an immediate right curl turn back to Main Street. Turn left on Main Street and go .3 miles, then bear right at the fork in the road onto Ipswich. Go about

Smith Farmhouse Marker

one-half mile and turn left on North Street. Go one-tenth

Original Smith Well

mile and turn left onto Boardman Street (stay on the right side of the forked road). Go to the end of the street and the home will be the last one on your left (Walker Road begins on your right). The home is privately owned and not available for tours.

- **Pine Grove Cemetery** – Many members of the Smith family are buried in this cemetery including Robert Smith, Samuel and his wife Rebecca, and Samuel Smith Jr. and his wife Priscilla. The exact locations of the graves are unknown but a memorial marker to the Smith family was erected under the supervision of George A. Smith in 1873. To go to the cemetery from the Smith farmhouse site, turn around and go back to North Street. Turn right on North Street and right on Ipswich. At the stop sign, make a sharp right turn onto Main Street/ Highway 97 North. The entrance to the cemetery will be on your left. As you enter the cemetery, the Smith family marker is located at your far left, very close to both a rock wall and the road (97 N.).

Smith Family Marker

Notes

_____

_____

_____

_____

_____

_____

_____

_____

_____

_____

_____

_____

_____

_____

_____

_____

_____

_____

Notes

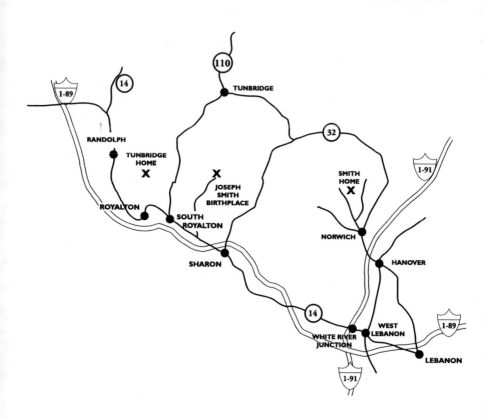

Chapter Four
Sharon

In the Bible, the Plain of Sharon (located north of Joppa) was known for its beauty and fertile land (see first Bible map in the LDS scriptures). Here a young David watched over his sheep prior to facing his adversary Goliath. Sharon, Vermont, bordering the White River, can also be described as a beautiful and fertile land. Chartered in 1761, it has a current population of about 1,400. Early settlers probably named the village after their previous home of Sharon, Connecticut.

In 1804, Solomon Mack purchased a 100-acre farm bordering the Royalton-Sharon Townships for the sum of $800. Soon after, he rented his cabin and about 68 acres of the farm to his daughter Lucy, her husband Joseph Smith Sr., and their four small children. On December 23, 1805, Lucy gave birth to a third son who was given the name of his father – Joseph Smith. Though the usual custom was to give the father's name to the oldest son, the naming of this young son fulfilled the prophecy made by another Joseph, who was sold into Egypt (2 Nephi 3:14-15). Like young David from the Plains of Sharon, young Joseph from the Township of Sharon would soon be challenged by and ultimately overcome his own adversities or "Goliaths."

PLANNING YOUR TIME

I suggest that you give yourself at least a full day for this area. Many have stopped only at the Joseph Smith Memorial and traveled on. Big Mistake! There are several other significant sites to visit and interesting stories to consider.

Besides the monument and surrounding sites at the Joseph Smith Memorial, suggested stops are included in the nearby areas of Royalton, Tunbridge, Norwich, and West Lebanon. If time allows, consider a stop at the granite quarry in Barre located about 25 miles further north, visit a nearby farm for a maple syrup demonstration, or enjoy the quaint villages of Woodstock and Quechee. For Vermont tourism questions, call 800-Vermont or call 888-848-4199 for questions about the Eastern Vermont area (includes Sharon).

GETTING THERE

Driving on I-89, take exit #2 for the Joseph Smith Memorial. After exiting, turn onto Route 132 towards Sharon. At the stop sign turn right onto Route 14. Continue on Route 14 (through the Village of Sharon) for about 4 miles until you see the Joseph Smith Memorial marker. Turn right onto Dairy Hill Road. The entrance to the Joseph Smith Memorial will be about 2 miles further on your right. While on Dairy Hill Road, you will pass two farms selling maple products. They are located on your right and just across the street from a John Deere business.

SIGNIFICANT EVENTS

After selling their farm in nearby Tunbridge, Joseph Sr. and Lucy lived briefly in Royalton before renting the log cabin and farm from Solomon Mack in Sharon Township. (The Village of Sharon is actually a few miles away). Lucy Smith recounts that during their three year stay, Joseph Sr. farmed the land in the summer and also taught school in the winter "during which time our circumstances gradually improved until we found ourselves quite comfortable again" (HJS p. 62). In 1807, the

Smith family moved back to Tunbridge, next to Royalton, then to West Lebanon, New Hampshire, and finally to Norwich, before leaving Vermont for the state of New York.

The birth of Lucy's fifth child, Joseph Smith Jr., on December 23, 1805 was not only a blessing to the family but also to the world. Though all that remains of his first home is the fireplace hearthstone and a stone from the front doorstep, a stately 38 1/2 foot high granite memorial honors this revered Prophet. The Church purchased the original Solomon Mack farm as well as much of the surrounding acreage in 1905. A small memorial cottage was originally built at this location but has since been replaced by a visitors' center. The impressive granite monument was dedicated on December 23, 1905 to commemorate the one-hundredth anniversary of Joseph's birth. President Joseph F. Smith, nephew of the Prophet and also one of our latter-day prophets, presided over the service and gave the dedicatory prayer. In his remarks, President Smith prayed that those who visited the monument would have a feeling of peace and "respect in their hearts" and that it would cause many "to reflect soberly upon this great problem of human life and redemption that has been opened up to the world through the instrumentality of the Prophet Joseph Smith" *(Proceedings at the Dedication of the Joseph Smith Memorial Monument, p. 26).*

SITES TO SEE

After entering the main gates of the Joseph Smith Memorial, you will first pass the LDS chapel on your left. Continue further and you will see the monument nestled on a rise between two buildings. The building on the right is the visitors' center while the building on the left houses the director. Directly behind the center is a road that makes a loop taking you past the Solomon Mack home site, the Daniel

Mack home site, and a small stone bridge. (The one-mile loop can be made by car or by foot.) The homes and bridge were located by what was once the old turnpike road. It was the main highway on which the Mack family traveled. You can still see remnants of the rock wall that once lined both sides of the road. Allow 1-2 hours if you are planning to see all of these sites at the memorial. A wonderful stop for children is at Camp Joseph located just minutes from the monument (see camping). It includes a playground, lots of grass, picnic tables, and a beautiful scenic view of the area.

- **LDS Visitors' Center** – Outside the center, notice the pictures showing the challenging process of bringing the monument from the quarry to its present site. Inside, notice the scale map of the Solomon Mack farm, the original hearthstone from the Smith family cottage, a rocking chair made by the young prophet, and a large bronze statue of Joseph Smith. In the 36-seat theater, you can watch one of several videos including "Joseph Smith – Prophet of the Restoration." Restrooms are located here. Allow at least 30-45 minutes for the free guided tour of the visitors' center and the monument. The beautiful grounds and picnic area make this a great lunch stop. Located at 357 LDS Lane, just off Dairy Hill Road. Open Monday thru Saturday 9 a.m.–7 p.m. and Sunday 1:30 p.m.–7 p.m. (May–Oct.). Winter hours are Monday thru Saturday 9 a.m.–5 p.m. and Sunday 1:30 p.m.–5 p.m. (Nov. – April). For more information call 802-763-7742.

- **Joseph Smith Monument** – Quarried at nearby Barre, this 38 1/2 foot single piece of granite, weighing about 39 tons, stands as a stately monument to the Prophet. Obelisk shaped, its height represents Joseph's age at the time of his martyrdom – 38 1/2 years. But standing on a base, with an additional ornamental top, the monument actually rises to over 50 feet high. Transporting the granite monument from Barre was difficult. The last 5 miles from South Royalton to the monument site were extremely challenging. In answer to prayers, the task of pulling this shaft

Joseph Smith Monument

over 5 miles of muddy roads by 2 oxen and 22 horses was finally accomplished when the ground froze. The monument was completed just days before the scheduled dedication date of December 23, 1905. Walk around the monument and take time to read the inscriptions on each side. Don't forget to take a picture with the sun reflecting off the top of the monument (see Photo Spots).

- **Log Cabin Site** – The birth site of the Prophet Joseph Smith is just to the left of the monument. The hearthstone originally located in the cabin can now be found inside the visitors' center. All that remains of the original cabin is the front doorstep of the home. Though Joseph's birthplace is generally considered as being in the Sharon Township, the home site actually straddled the boundary between the Royalton and Sharon Townships, with portions of the

Log Cabin Site

home in each township. Years ago, a Memorial Cottage marked the site of the Prophet's birthplace. The birdhouse located just to the left of the cabin site was built by one of the missionaries and is a replica of this cottage.

- **Solomon Mack Home Site** – A marker at this site reads, "The Solomon Mack Farm. 100 acres was purchased by him in 1804. An extra house on it was rented to his son-in-law Joseph Smith Sr. This old cellar is all that remains of the Solomon Mack home. Near by may be seen foundations for the out buildings." Solomon and Lydia Gates Mack were the parents of Lucy Smith (the Prophet's mother). Solomon was born in Lyme, Connecticut on September 15, 1732. Apprenticed to a farmer at a young age, he enlisted in the service of King George II at the age of 21 and fought in the French and Indian War. He later met and married an "accomplished young woman" and schoolteacher – Lydia Gates. Credited as having an "excellent disposition," she provided her children with a strong educational and spiritual upbringing (see CHC 1:19). Their third daughter,

Solomon Mack Home Site

Lucy, would also provide this same educational and spiritual training for her own children.

- **Old Stone Bridge** – A marker reads, "This bridge is typical of the early small bridges in New England. It is made entirely of stones and was here before 1804, when the Solomon Mack family purchased the farm. The old turnpike which was the main highway through this country crossed this bridge at that time."

- **Daniel G. Mack Home Site** –A marker at this site reads, "This old cellar and foundation mark the spot where the Daniel Mack family probably lived for many years after the Solomon Mack farm was sold by Daniel's father in 1811. Lydia Gates Mack, the mother of Daniel and Lucy Mack Smith, lived here with Daniel until her death about 1817." Lucy describes her brother Daniel as "a man of the world." She also described him as one who was "always the first to the rescue." Daniel once risked his own life to save three men who were drowning (HJS p. 31). In her later years, Lydia Mack lived with her daughter Lucy's family until their move to Palmyra. Lydia then moved in with her son Daniel. She died around 1817 from injuries she received in a wagon accident (HJS p. 84).

- **School House** – Tradition says that the red brick home located just to the left and across the street from the entrance to the Joseph Smith Memorial is the actual school where Joseph Smith Sr. taught. The home is privately owned and not available for tours.

THINGS TO DO

- **Hike to the top of Patriarch Hill** – The trail to the top of the hill starts from the Joseph Smith Memorial visitors' center. Allow yourself at least an hour for the moderate hike up the hill. Enjoy the beautiful vista from the top and don't forget to see Patriarch Tree – it is over 200 years old.

- Enjoy the live nativity and over 100,000 lights decorating the monument and the surrounding area during the month of December. Call the visitors' center for more information.

- **Sugarbush Farm** – Visit a small working farm and learn about the process of making maple syrup. Enjoy free samples of syrup and cheese, beautiful scenery, a nature walk, and an educational maple sugar display. Admission is free. Open year round 9 a.m.–5 p.m. Show this book to receive a 10% discount at the gift store. (We can't go home without their extra sharp cheddar!) The farm is located 15 miles from Sharon, and about a 30 minute drive. It is situated between Woodstock and Quechee at 591 Sugarbush Farm Road. For directions and further info, visit www.sugarbushfarm.com or call 800-281-1757. (In winter and early spring, call ahead to check for store hours and road conditions.) **D**

- **Rock of Ages Granite Quarries in Barre** – Stop in the quarry visitors' center and see the free video explaining the quarrying process, visit the excavation site next to the center where the Joseph Smith monument was quarried

Granite Quarry

(currently inactive), take home a free sample of granite available at this quarry, or take a 35 minute shuttle bus tour of the upper quarry. Admission: (for bus tour only) children/$2 and adults/$4.50. Open May thru October 8:30 a.m.–5 p.m. (last bus tour at 3:30). Located about 25 miles north of Sharon. Traveling on I-89 north, take exit #6. After exiting stay on Route 63 to the bottom of the hill, go through the light, and follow the signs. 802-476-3119.

- **Quechee Gorge** – Visit the Quechee Gorge overlook sometimes referred to as Vermont's Little Grand Canyon (165 ft. deep). Bike paths and hiking trails are located at the Quechee Gorge State Park. Located off I-89 (exit #1) on Route 4.

PHOTO SPOTS

- **Joseph Smith Monument** – You can get a unique shot of the monument if you catch the sun reflecting off the top. (This shot is worth waiting for the clouds to part!) In the dedicatory prayer, Joseph F. Smith dedicated the spire as "a token of the inspired man of God whom thou didst make indeed a polished shaft in thine hand, reflecting the light of heaven, even thy glorious light, unto the children of men" (*ERA* Feb. 1906, pp. 324 – 325).

Joseph Smith Monument

- The local scenery is picture perfect, especially if you are visiting in the fall and able to catch the fall foliage. But don't leave this area during any season without a shot of at least one of New England's famous covered bridges or white-framed churches.

LDS CHURCH SERVICES

The South Royalton Ward meets in the chapel located at the Joseph Smith Memorial (175 LDS Lane) at 10 a.m. Check the Church web site at www.lds.org to verify current meeting times.

ATM

An ATM machine is conveniently located next to the Sharon Trading Post. You will find it just after exiting I-89 and making a right turn onto Route 14. Additional ATM locations are mentioned in other chapters.

SHOPPING

- **Sharon Trading Post** – A quaint little country store complete with small souvenir items, maple syrup products, and deli with made to order sandwiches. Located on Route 14. 802-763-7404.

- **Quechee** – In a picture perfect setting, this area offers a wide variety of shopping options including antique stores, New England candle shops, glass novelties, and many Vermont specialty stores. Pizza parlors, diners, and other restaurants are also located here. Located off I-89 (exit # 1) on Route 4.

- **Woodstock** – Located near Quechee, this area also has many art, pottery, glass, and Vermont specialty stores. Numerous eating and lodging choices are nearby. From Quechee, continue on Route 4 through Taftsville and into Woodstock.

RESTAURANTS

There is a wide range of dining choices including fast food, country cooking, and fine dining. We have tried to include many choices in and around this area. Some are listed in this chapter, while others are mentioned in other chapters (Royalton, West Lebanon, etc.).

WHITE RIVER JUNCTION

- **A. J.'s Steakhouse** – Located just past the Comfort Inn on 40 Bowling Lane. 802-295-3071.

- **McDonald's** – Located at 1 Beswick Drive.

- **Crossroad Café** – Local favorite for breakfast. Located at 96 Sykes Ave. 802-295-9484.

WEST LEBANON

The largest variety of restaurants is here; see West Lebanon chapter for a detailed list.

HANOVER

Hanover is a popular college town (Dartmouth College) and offers many fast food and fine dining choices. Local favorites include:

- **Ben & Jerry's Ice Cream** – You have to have at least one cone while in Vermont. Located just across the street from Dartmouth College.

- **Molly's Restaurant** – Offering pizza, pasta, sandwiches, etc. Located at 43 South Main. 603-643-2570.

- **Jesse's Steak & Seafood** – Located on Route 120. 603-643-4111.

LODGING

There are very few lodging choices in Sharon itself; most are found in the surrounding area. Advance reservations are suggested, especially during the fall foliage season.

SHARON

- **Baxter Mountain House B&B** – Relax and enjoy the country air in this Gambrel-style home on a quiet dirt road. Main floor guest room w/queen bed and private bath at $85 and two upstairs guest rooms w/shared bath at $70 (year-round). Full breakfast is included. Located about ten minutes from the Joseph Smith Monument at 1298 Fay Brook Road. Contact Nancy and Ken at 802-763-8824 **D**

WHITE RIVER JUNCTION

Located about 13 miles south of the Joseph Smith Memorial at the junction of I-89 and I-91, White River Junction offers the largest selection of lodging choices.

- **Comfort Suites** – Conveniently located near the Joseph Smith Memorial (15 miles), Dartmouth College (5 miles), and Quechee Gorge (4 miles). Built in 2003, this hotel has 68 rooms, all non-smoking and each with microwave and fridge. Amenities include a fitness center, business center, laundry facilities and shared pool (with Hampton Inn). Located at 102 Ballardvale Drive. 802-291-9911. **D**

- **Comfort Inn** – Select from 95 rooms or junior suites, starting at $89, with continental breakfast included. Also features indoor pool and fitness room. Located at 8 Sykes Mountain Avenue. 802-295-3051. **D**

- **Holiday Inn Express** – Located at 121 Ballardvale Drive. 802-299-2700.

- **Hampton Inn** – Nice hotel with indoor pool and health club. Located at 105 Ballardvale Drive. 802-296-2800.

- **Super 8 Motel** – 83 Rooms with access to indoor pool and hot tub. 802-295-7577.

WEST LEBANON

- **Fireside Inn and Suites** – Featuring 126 rooms, on-site restaurant, fitness center, and indoor pool. Located at 25 Airport Road. 603-298-5900.

LEBANON

- **Courtyard by Marriott** – Built in 2006, this non smoking property features 124 rooms. Located at 10 Morgan Drive. 603-643-5600.

- **Marriott Residence Inn** – 114 rooms, many of them non-smoking. Includes deluxe continental breakfast, indoor pool and exercise room. 603-643-4511.

HANOVER

- **Chieftain Inn** – 22 rooms with continental breakfast included. 603-643-2550.

- **The Hanover Inn** – Full-service hotel featuring deluxe accommodations w/on-site restaurants. Located across the square from Dartmouth College. 800-443-7024.

QUECHEE

Located about 15 miles from Sharon; traveling on I-89, take exit #1 and follow Route 4 into town.

- **Quality Inn** – Located near the Quechee Gorge, with outdoor pool and on-site restaurant. 800-732-4376.

- **Quechee Inn at Marshland Farms** – Nice accommodations with on-site restaurant. 25 rooms, with breakfast included. 800-235-3133.

CAMPING

- **Camp Joseph** – Owned and operated by the local LDS stake, Camp Joseph is a wonderful camping spot or family reunion site (no RV hookups). Featuring 15 cabins (10' by 10') with two bunk beds priced at $15/night, per cabin (sleeps four, no electricity and bring your own sleeping bags), camping sites at $5/night, pavilion, swing set, picnic tables, clubhouse, volleyball and horseshoe area. Open May thru October. Located just past the Joseph Smith Memorial on Dairy Hill Road. Make your reservations early by calling 802-563-3317 or contact the visitors' center.

- **Quechee Valley KOA** – Situated in a beautiful wooded setting, this RV resort features over 90 sites with electricity, laundromat, picnic tables, bathhouse w/hot showers, swimming pool, playground, and on-site store. Open from late April thru late October. Located just off I-89 (exit #1) on Route 4 near Quechee. 802-296-6711.

Notes

Notes

_____

_____

_____

_____

_____

_____

_____

_____

_____

_____

_____

_____

_____

_____

_____

_____

_____

_____

Notes

Notes

_____

_____

_____

_____

_____

_____

_____

_____

_____

_____

_____

_____

_____

_____

_____

_____

_____

_____

Notes

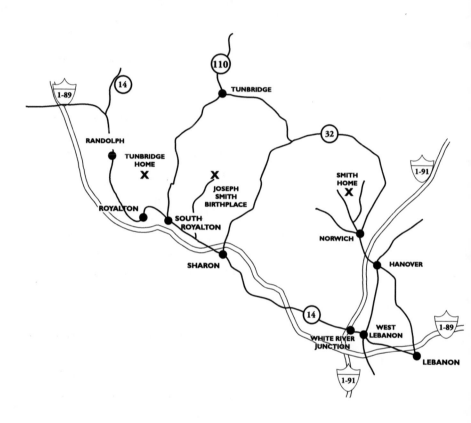

Chapter Five
Tunbridge

The Township of Tunbridge is located about 8 miles northwest of Sharon and has a current population of about 1,300. Within the township are three small villages: Tunbridge, South Tunbridge and North Tunbridge. First chartered in 1761, Tunbridge was officially organized in 1786 (after the Revolutionary War) and was probably named after Viscount Tunbridge, a prominent British friend of Benning Wentworth, the royal governor of New Hampshire. Tunbridge became somewhat of a resort in the 1800s due to the locally discovered mineral springs. Many visitors now come to enjoy the beautiful countryside and to attend the annual Tunbridge Fair, usually held during the second week in September.

More significant for Latter-day Saints is the fact that for almost 25 years, this area was home to both sides of Joseph Smith's lineage: the Smiths and the Macks. Joseph's paternal grandfather, Asael Smith, moved to Tunbridge in 1791 and his maternal grandfather, Solomon Mack, arrived a few years later in 1799. Lucy probably met her future husband here while working in her brother's store. She and Joseph Smith Sr. were married on January 24, 1796 and lived here on three different occasions. In Tunbridge, Lucy gave birth to her first child, a son who died at birth, as well as four of her nine children who lived to adulthood: Alvin, Hyrum, Sophronia, and Samuel.

PLANNING YOUR TIME

If time is short, spend a few minutes and stop at the village store where tradition says Lucy first met Joseph Sr. If time allows: stop at the town clerk's office to see their marriage entry, visit the Hutchinson Cemetery to see John Mudget's grave, or drive through the general area of "Tunbridge Gore" where Joseph Sr. and Lucy lived.

GETTING THERE

As you leave the Joseph Smith Memorial, turn right onto Route 14 and head north for about 1 mile. After entering South Royalton, turn right at the junction of Route 14 and Route 110. The Tunbridge Village Store is located on the right side of Route 110 about 5.7 miles from the junction.

SIGNIFICANT EVENTS

Asael Smith moved his wife, Mary Duty, and their eleven children from Massachusetts to Tunbridge in the spring of 1791. Asael's two oldest boys, Jesse and Joseph Sr., were sent ahead to clear the land and build a small cabin. Asael initially purchased about 83 acres but he later bought additional land and eventually owned over 350 acres. Asael lived here for over 20 years before moving to Stockholm, New York. Both Jesse and Joseph Sr. had property near their father's land.

Lucy Mack was born and raised in Gilsum, New Hampshire. Her older brother Stephen had once promised his mother that he would always look after his younger sister, Lucy, who was then just 8 years old. (Their mother was very ill at the time the promise was made and she thought she might not live.) Less than 10 years later, Stephen, who was now living in Tunbridge, visited his family home and convinced his parents to let him take Lucy back to live with him. She was ill in health and spirits, grieving over the death of her sister Lovina. During this difficult period, Lucy spent much of her time reading the Bible, praying, and pondering. While working at Stephen's store, she met a young man by the name of Joseph Smith (HJS p. 42). Lucy lived with her brother for a year, went back to her family home for a few months, and then returned to live with Stephen "and was with him until the ensuing January when I was married" (HJS p. 42). Lucy was twenty when she and twenty-four year old Joseph Smith Sr. were married on January 24, 1796. This marriage lasted forty-four years until the death of Joseph Sr. in 1840.

Joseph Sr. and Lucy lived in Tunbridge for the first 6 years of their marriage. During this time they had two sons, Alvin and Hyrum. Joseph owned "a handsome farm" and supported his young family by "tilling the earth." After six years, they rented out the farm in 1802 and relocated to the nearby town of Randolph. Later that same year, after Joseph's new business venture failed, the family returned to their Tunbridge farm. Their daughter Sophronia was born here before they moved again – first to Royalton and then to Sharon where another son was born, Joseph Smith Jr. The Smith family would return one last time to Tunbridge where another son, Samuel Harrison, was born on March 13, 1811. Their stay in Tunbridge was short before moving to Royalton.

Though Lucy faced several challenges in her early years of marriage including frequent moving, illness, and a failed business venture, she also had many special experiences. One such experience occurred here. "While, we were yet living in the town of Tunbridge, my mind became deeply impressed with the subject of religion" (HJS p. 58). Concerned that her husband did not share this same interest, she retired to a nearby grove and prayed that her husband might also become more "religiously inclined." Upon returning home, Lucy had a powerful dream after which she felt certain that her husband would hear and eventually accept the "undefiled gospel of the Son of God" (HJS p. 60). Lucy would live to see her dream fulfilled.

SITES TO SEE

Credit for the location of many of the sites in Tunbridge and surrounding areas goes to local historian Lester Corwin, who passed away in October of 2007. We express great appreciation for his help in locating the sites and for sharing his extensive knowledge of the area. He is missed.

The Village Store

- **The Village Store** – Originally called the "Mack and Mudget Store;" Lucy once worked at this store then owned by her brother, Stephen Mack, and his partner,

John Mudget. As you look at this small country store, you can almost imagine Lucy meeting Joseph Smith Sr. here for the first time. Unfortunately, the store has recently closed and future plans for the building are uncertain at this time. However, I suggest you still stop to take pictures. It is located at 302 Route 110, about 5.7 miles from the junction of Routes 14/110.

- **Tunbridge Town Clerk's Office** – For those interested in viewing historical records, the marriage entry of Joseph Sr. and Lucy on January 24, 1797 (performed by Seth Austin, Justice of the Peace) can be found in Volume A (1782 – 1809 Proprietors' Record) on page 129. The birth entry of Alvin is on page 130. The clerk's office is located on your left about 5.2 miles from the Route 14/110 junction (and just south of the Tunbridge Village Store) at 271 Route 110.

- **Hutchinson Cemetery** – The grave of John Mudget, business partner of Stephen Mack, is located in this small cemetery. During a discussion concerning a wedding present for Lucy, John Mudget commented to Stephen "Lucy ought to have something worth naming, and I will give her just as much as you will." To this, Stephen replied "I will give her five hundred dollars in cash." John replied, "Good, and I will give her five hundred dollars more" (HJS p. 44). Lucy would later have to use this money to help pay debts created by the failure of their business venture. To locate this small cemetery after visiting the store, go 1 mile west on Route 110 (heading towards the junction) and turn right on Howe Lane. You will see the cemetery almost immediately on your right. To find John Mudget's grave, pass through

John Mudget Headstone
(middle stone)

the gate and then to the right just behind the cemetery sign. Walk straight east behind the sign to the middle of the cemetery, turn to your right and walk about 25 feet straight south. The dark charcoal slate headstone will be facing you.

- **Birth Site of Alvin, Hyrum, and Sophronia Smith** – Visit the site of the Smith home in "Tunbridge Gore" after stopping at the Hutchinson Cemetery. (This is an unpaved road, I would not recommend going if the road is muddy. Also not suggested for any vehicle larger than a van.) From the Hutchinson Cemetery, continue on Howe Lane and drive through the covered bridge. At 0.2 of a mile, bear right at the fork in the road onto Falls Hill Road. Continue about a mile and at the next fork in the road, bear left at the red Tunbridge schoolhouse. After going 3.5 miles from the cemetery, you will come to a sign on your right that says Johnson Circle. Do not take

Hyrum Smith Birth Site

this road but continue 0.1 mile further. Stop here to see the small depression immediately next to the road on your right. A large rectangular fenced garden plot w/scarecrow is directly behind the site. (Watch out for poison ivy.) Tradition and local historian Lester Corwin agree that this was the location of the Smith family home. The small sunken area is the site of the foundation. Continue on another 3.2 miles to return to Route 110 (bearing left at the fork in the road). Turning right onto 110 will take you to the Route 14/110 junction at South Royalton. Turning left onto Route 110 takes you to Tunbridge.

Notes

_____

_____

_____

_____

_____

_____

_____

_____

_____

_____

_____

_____

_____

_____

_____

_____

_____

_____

Notes

Chapter Six
Royalton

The Township of Royalton, just west of the Township of Sharon, was chartered in 1769. With a current population of about 2,600, the township contains three villages: Royalton, North Royalton, and South Royalton. Lucy's father, Solomon Mack, purchased a 100-acre farm in this area. He lived on the portion of land in the Township of Sharon, but his property lay in both townships. Joseph Sr. and Lucy lived in the Royalton area on two separate occasions. After selling their home in Tunbridge, the family lived here for a few months before moving to Sharon. During their second stay in Royalton, from about 1809 to 1811, Lucy gave birth to two sons, Ephraim and William. In 1816, Lucy bade a tearful farewell to her mother, Lydia Gates Mack, as Lucy and the children departed for their new home in Palmyra. Lydia died in Royalton about two years later. Stephen Smith, brother of Joseph Smith Sr., is buried in the small local cemetery.

PLANNING YOUR TIME

Though most will not want to make Royalton a planned stop, you will likely pass through this area on your way to the Tunbridge Village Store. Knowing about some of the things that transpired here will help make this area more meaningful to you.

GETTING THERE

South Royalton is located 3.2 miles from the Joseph Smith Memorial. After leaving the visitors' center, return to Route 14 and turn right. You will see the town sign just before the junction of Route 14 and Route 110. To find South Royalton, turn left at this junction and cross the South Royalton Bridge into the main square. Royalton is about two miles further on Route 14.

SIGNIFICANT EVENTS

After selling their farm in Tunbridge to pay off the debts from a failed business venture, Joseph Sr. and Lucy moved to Royalton for a few months before continuing on to Sharon. During a later stay in this area, Lucy gave birth to Ephraim on March 13, 1810 and William exactly a year later on March 13, 1811. Sadly, Ephraim only lived for 11 days before passing away on March 24, 1810.

Around the time of William's birth in 1811, Joseph Sr. had a remarkable dream which would be the first of several he would experience over the next few years. Of this dream, Lucy recorded, "One night my husband retired to his bed in a very thoughtful state of mind, contemplating the situation of the Christian religion, or the confusion and discord that were extant. He soon fell into a sleep, and before waking had the following vision ..." (HJS p. 63). In this dream, Joseph Sr. found himself traveling through a silent, dismal, and barren field, which represented the world without any religion. He was told about a log box which contained food that when eaten would make him wise. His attempts to eat some of the food were prevented by beasts. Joseph awoke trembling but happy and even more convinced than ever that the professors of religion did not understand the kingdom of God. (Joseph Sr. would soon have a second such dream after moving from Royalton to West Lebanon.)

In 1816, Lucy last saw her mother at the home of Willard Pierce, a tavern keeper in Royalton. Lydia wept as she told her daughter that she would probably never see her face again. Lydia encouraged her daughter to "continue faithful in the exercise of every religious duty to the end of your days, that I may have the pleasure of embracing you in another, fairer world above" (HJS p. 84). After Lucy had departed for Palmyra, Lydia lived with her son, Daniel Mack, for two years until she passed away.

SITES TO SEE

- **Site of Pierce Tavern** – A privately owned home (not the original) now stands at the site where Lucy probably said a final goodbye to her mother. The tavern site is located

Pierce Tavern Site

on the corner at the intersection of Route 14 and Route 110 (on your left as you turn onto Route 110 to see the Tunbridge Village Store).

- **North Royalton Cemetery** – The grave of the Prophet's uncle, Stephen Smith, is located in this small cemetery. The cemetery is on your left about 3 miles north of the Route 14/110 junction (or 0.2 miles south of the Fox Stand Inn on Route 14). A rock wall divides the graveyard. Stephen's round-shaped headstone is in the south section midway between the dividing rock wall and the southern boundary. The black slate stone is in the third row from the front (the writing is on the backside).

Stephen Smith Headstone

- **Fox Stand Inn** – The inn is of historical interest because General Lafayette stopped here after the American Revolution while returning from Montreal. The building is located on Route 14.

- Royalton was also the birthplace of **Albert Carrington**. He was born on January 8, 1813 and graduated from Dartmouth College. He served as an apostle from 1870 to 1885. Though he left the Church for a time, Albert Carrington was later rebaptized and served on a committee that helped draft a constitution for the state of Utah.

ATM

The Randolph National Bank (with ATM) is situated on the square in South Royalton.

SHOPPING

• Many locally produced maple sugar products and Vermont souvenirs are sold in the country store at Eaton's Sugarhouse (see restaurants).

• Enjoy the Farmer's Market held every Saturday morning on the green from mid-May thru mid-October (middle of the square in South Royalton).

RESTAURANTS

• **Royalton Village Pizza** – Features sandwiches, pizza, salads, pasta, and calzones. We enjoyed our pizza and found it reasonably priced. Open daily 11 a.m.–9 p.m. Located near Eaton's on Route 14. 802-763-2800.

• **Eaton's Sugarhouse** – Serves both breakfast and lunch, with a wide variety of homemade choices. Sample a free piece of maple candy made on-site. Also includes an antique and country store. Open daily 7 a.m.–3 p.m. Located close to Royalton Village Pizza at the junction of Route 14 and Route 107. 802-763-8809 or 1-888-VTMAPLE.

• There are several other eating places located at the square in South Royalton. These include: RB's Delicatessen, Pizza/Deli, and Chelsea's Station.

Notes

Notes

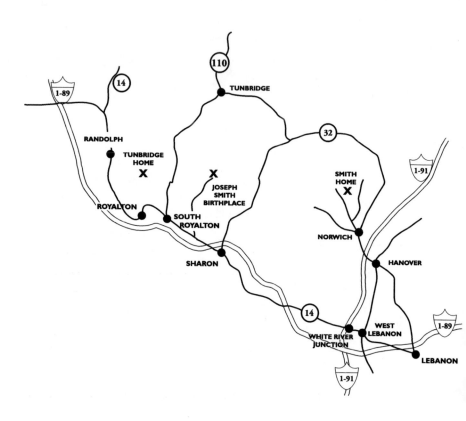

Chapter Seven
Randolph

The Township of Randolph was named after Edmund Randolph and received its charter in 1781. Edmund was a delegate to the Constitutional Congress but declined to sign the constitution because he felt it was not republican enough. Randolph was also the home of Justin Morgan, who is remembered as the breeder of the remarkable Morgan horse. The town currently has a population of about 5,000 and is located about 10 miles northwest of South Royalton.

Randolph marks a brief but eventful period in the early marriage of Joseph Sr. and Lucy. Though the exact location of their store and home is unknown, it is helpful to learn about some of the significant events that occurred here. (Some of the local historians feel the store was once located near the current intersection of Route 14 and Clay Wight Hill Road.)

SIGNIFICANT EVENTS

Joseph Smith Sr. and Lucy rented out their farm in Tunbridge and moved to Randolph where they opened a mercantile store in 1802. Their small family consisted of Joseph Sr., Lucy and their two sons: Alvin and Hyrum. After living here for less than six months, Lucy became very ill with tuberculosis. Told by doctors that she would not live, she made a covenant with the Lord "that if He would let me live, I would endeavor to get that religion that would enable me to serve him right, whether it was in the Bible or wherever it might be found" (HJS p. 48). Lucy's health quickly improved and for the rest of her life she kept her promise to serve the Lord to the best of her ability.

Unfortunately, Joseph Sr.'s business venture was not successful. At the time of their family move, Randolph was one of the larger villages in the state and the store seemed to be a sound business venture. Joseph Sr. also became interested in crystallizing and exporting ginseng root to China where it was in great demand as a remedy for the plague. Due to the dishonesty of Mr. Stevens (a business associate), Joseph Sr. did not receive the full proceeds from the sale of his ginseng root shipment. Telling Joseph Sr. that the sale in China had been a failure, Mr. Stevens took the large amount of silver and gold received from the actual sale of the ginseng and fled to Canada. Joseph Sr. was left heavily in debt, having borrowed money for store goods with plans to pay the debt from the proceeds of his shipment to China. He now owed about $1,800. Joseph Sr. and Lucy were able to pay off their debt by using the $1,000 given to them as a wedding present and by selling their farm in Tunbridge at only half its value (HJS p. 53). Then debt-free but struggling financially, the young Smith family moved to Royalton and soon after relocated to Sharon on the farm of Lucy's father.

Notes

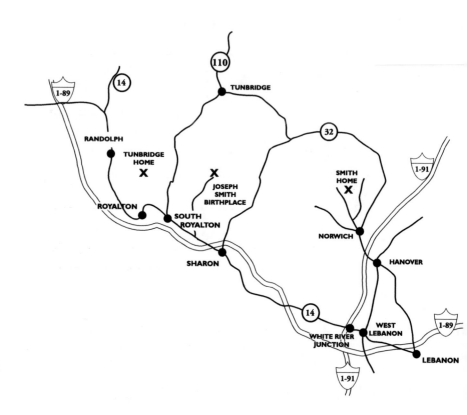

Chapter Eight
West Lebanon

West Lebanon, New Hampshire was established in 1761 and is located close to the Vermont border. Less than 5 miles away in Hanover stood Moor's Academy which was adjacent to Dartmouth College. Dr. Nathan Smith, founder and professor at Dartmouth Medical School (no relation to Joseph), would become very important to Joseph Smith and his family after their move to this area.

In 1811, Joseph Smith Sr. moved his family from Royalton, Vermont into a rented home here in West Lebanon, New Hampshire. Not long after their arrival, Joseph Sr. received a vision very similar to the tree of life vision recorded in the Book of Mormon (HJS pp. 64-66). Here too, they were blessed with the birth of their second daughter, Katherine, in July 1812. She was the ninth of eleven children born to Joseph Sr. and Lucy. During their two-year stay, Hyrum, their second son, attended Moor's Academy while the rest of their school-age children attended a nearby school.

The Smith children became ill with the typhus fever that ravaged the entire area in 1813 and took over 6,000 lives. Though all of the children eventually recovered, young Joseph developed a painful secondary infection that settled in his leg. After several unsuccessful attempts to contain the infection, doctors wanted to amputate his leg. Lucy pleaded with the surgeons to make one last attempt. That Dr. Nathan Smith, a surgeon who pioneered the medical procedure needed to save Joseph's leg, was at nearby Dartmouth College was very providential. Joseph underwent the painful operation without anesthesia and though he would ever after walk with a slight limp, his leg was saved.

PLANNING YOUR TIME

This is a very brief but meaningful stop. The site where the Smith family home was once located is just seconds from the freeway exit. Take a brief rest stop to drive to the site and discuss Joseph's miraculous operation. If you are looking for dining choices, the largest variety of restaurants for the Sharon area is located in this vicinity.

GETTING THERE

Driving on I-89: take exit #20. (If traveling east, take exit #20, turn left and cross under the freeway.) After exiting, turn right onto 12 A. You will almost immediately come to a signal with Shaw's Plaza on your right. Turn right at this intersection and you will see a KFC/Taco Bell almost immediately on your left. This is the site where the rented home of the Smith family once stood.

Driving on I-91: take the I-89 West Lebanon/Concord exit and then continue on to exit #20.

SIGNIFICANT EVENTS

Lucy Mack Smith, mother of the Prophet Joseph Smith, tells in the *History of Joseph Smith by His Mother* of the anguish she experienced when all of her children were struck with typhus fever. Sophronia was the first child who became ill, but soon Hyrum, Alvin, and then all of the other children became sick. The doctor attending Sophronia gave up hope that she would recover after taking care of her for eighty-nine days. As she lay almost lifeless, Joseph Sr. knelt at her bedside and prayed that his daughter's life might be spared. With a testimony that she would recover, Lucy paced the floor tightly holding her daughter. After finally hearing Sophronia utter a few sobs and seeing that her breathing was less labored, Lucy collapsed on the bed with her daughter, overcome by both emotion and exhaustion. Sophronia did recover (HJS pp. 69-71).

Seven year-old Joseph had only been ill for about two weeks with the typhus fever before he seemingly recovered. But soon he developed a severe pain in his shoulder. First dismissed as a sprain by the doctors, the pain persisted until the doctor discovered a large fever sore on his shoulder. "He immediately lanced it, upon which it discharged a full quart of matter"(HJS p. 72). Joseph continued to suffer as the infection traveled down his side and settled into the bone of his left leg. Lucy took care of her son for almost two weeks until she became ill herself from exhaustion. Joseph's old brother, Hyrum, took his mother's place and stayed by Joseph's side almost day and night, taking care of his brother and pressing down tightly on Joseph's leg to help relieve some of the pain.

After unsuccessful attempts were made to contain the infection by making incisions, the doctors determined that amputation of the leg was the only solution to save Joseph's life. Lucy pled with Dr. Nathan Smith, Dr. Stone, and several other doctors from Dartmouth Medical School to make one last attempt to save her son's leg. Doctor Smith finally agreed to perform an extremely complicated surgery. The doctors wanted to bind Joseph to the bed but Joseph objected. He also refused brandy or wine usually given to dull the pain of surgery. Instead he asked that his father hold him in his arms and that his mother leave the room so that she would not have to witness his suffering.

The rarely performed surgery consisted of boring into the bone on both sides and breaking out three infected portions. Hearing Joseph scream, Lucy burst into the room but left again at Joseph's urging. She reentered the room later to see "the wound torn open to view, my boy and the bed on which he lay covered with the blood that was still gushing from the wound" (HJS p. 75).

The surgery proved to be a success and Joseph was sent to stay with his Uncle Jesse Smith in Salem, Massachusetts with hopes that the sea air would speed his recovery. Joseph walked with the help of crutches for the next three years and had a slight limp for the rest of his life. The Smith family felt very blessed and acknowledged the Lord's hand in preserving Joseph's life.

SITES TO SEE

- **Smith Family Home Site** – Though the Smith family home was torn down in 1967, you can visit the site and discuss the events that occurred here. The rented home beside the Mascoma River once stood about where the KFC/Taco Bell is located in Shaw's Plaza.

- **Dartmouth College** – As previously mentioned, twelve year-old Hyrum Smith attended Moor's Academy that was once located adjacent to this college. Dr. Nathan Smith, one of Dartmouth's prominent medical professors, with the help of about 10 of his colleagues and medical students, performed the surgery that saved Joseph's leg and preserved his life. The college is located about 2 miles north of West Lebanon in the town of Hanover. To drive to Dartmouth, continue on 12 A until it runs into 10 N. Turn left onto 10 N. and continue into Hanover.

ATM

The closest ATM is located at Shaw's Market; additional banks are also located along 12 A.

RESTAURANTS

You will find the largest selection of restaurants in this area. Dining options are located on both sides of freeway exit #20.

Restaurants located on the north side of 12 A include:

At Shaw's Plaza (first signal on your right):

- **KFC/Taco Bell and Dunkin Donuts.**

- **Shaw's Market** – grocery store, deli, and salad bar.

At Power House Mall (second signal on your right):

- **Lui Lui** – Featuring pizza, pasta, calzones, salads, and many other choices. 603-298-7070.

At Glen Road Plaza (a little further on 12 A, on your right):

- **Subway and Domino's Pizza.**

Across from Shaw's Plaza (first signal on your left):

- **Chili's** – 10 Benning Street. 603-298-6991.

Restaurants located on the south side of the freeway on South Main include:

- **Weathervane** – New England seafood restaurant 603-298-7805.

- **Koto's Japanese Steakhouse and Sushi Bar** – 603-298-2925

- **Other choices include:** Friendly's, Applebee's, Panera Bread, Wendy's, McDonald's, Burger King, Pizza Hut, Denny's, and TCBY.

- **Wal-Mart** – This store has a grocery/convenience food section.

- **Price Chopper** – This grocery store is located next to Wal-Mart.

Notes

_____

_____

_____

_____

_____

_____

_____

_____

_____

_____

_____

_____

_____

_____

_____

_____

_____

_____

Notes

Notes

_____

_____

_____

_____

_____

_____

_____

_____

_____

_____

_____

_____

_____

_____

_____

_____

_____

_____

_____

Chapter Nine
Norwich

Originally spelled Norwhich, the Village of Norwich with a population of approximately 3,500 is located about 25 miles southeast of Sharon, close to the Vermont/New Hampshire border. In 1813, Joseph Smith Sr. and his family moved from West Lebanon, New Hampshire to a rented farm in Norwich, Vermont. Young Joseph Jr. was on crutches, still recovering from his leg surgery. During their three-year stay, the family was blessed by the birth of Don Carlos on March 25, 1816. Unfortunately, during those same three years the family financial situation continued to get worse. After experiencing a third consecutive year of crop failure, Joseph Smith Sr. decided to move his family and start over. In 1816, hearing about fertile and well-timbered land available in the state of New York, Joseph Sr. left to see for himself. He soon sent word for his wife and children to join him. Their destination for a new beginning was Palmyra, New York.

PLANNING YOUR TIME

This is a brief stop before or after visiting Dartmouth College or West Lebanon. We suggest you take a few minutes and drive by the home once rented by the Smith family before their final move from Vermont.

GETTING THERE

Traveling on I-89, take the White River Junction exit and travel north about 5 miles on I-91, to exit #13. Turn left after exiting and continue on Main Street into Norwich.

Traveling on I-91, take exit #13; turn left and follow Main Street into town.

Coming from Hanover (Dartmouth College), continue west on Route 120 and cross over the Connecticut River and into Norwich.

SIGNIFICANT EVENTS

Lucy recorded, "When health returned to us, it found us, as may well be supposed, in very low circumstances. Sickness, with all its attendant expenses of nurses, medical attendants, and other necessary articles, reduced us so that we were now compelled to make arrangements for going into some kind of business to provide for present wants, rather than future prospects...My husband now determined to change his residence. Accordingly, we moved to Norwich in Vermont and established on a farm belonging to Squire Moredock. The first year our crops failed, and we bought our bread with the proceeds of the orchard and our own industry" (HJS p. 81). Unfortunately, this crop failure was not their last. A second year in Norwich brought a second failed crop. Determined to try once more, Joseph Sr. planted again, hopeful that this year would be successful, unlike the previous two.

In Vermont history, the year of 1816 was sometimes referred to as "eighteen hundred and froze to death." Volcanic ash released from one of the world's largest volcanic eruptions at Mount Tambora in far away Indonesia resulted in weather-altering patterns throughout the world, including the New England states. The Smith family's crops froze, as did many others during the "year without a summer." As Lucy wrote, "This was enough. My husband was now altogether decided upon going to New York" (HJS pp. 81-82).

Deeply in debt, Joseph Sr. attempted to settle with all his creditors before moving his family. Believing all was in order, he left to investigate the state of New York, where "wheat was raised in abundance." Lucy soon received word from her husband to pack their belongings into the wagon and prepare to move. Joseph Sr. made arrangements for a team and driver to bring his family to their new home in Palmyra. As Lucy and her eight children were about to leave, a group of creditors presented additional claims. Ready to depart, Lucy concluded "it would be more to our advantage to pay their unjust claims than to hazard a lawsuit" (HJS p. 83). Not having the time to dispute the claims and refusing offers to raise money for her assistance, Lucy sold many of her possessions and was able to settle the debt of one hundred and fifty dollars by "considerable exertion."

Lucy and the children left Norwich on December 16, 1816 and in January 1817, they joyfully reunited with Joseph Sr. in their new hometown – Palmyra, New York.

SITES TO SEE

Smith Family Home

- **Smith Family Home** – The two-story home of Squire Murdock (or Moredock), which was rented by the Smith family, is privately owned and not available for tours. To find this home, drive north through the village of Norwich on Main Street for about 1 mile and turn left onto Turnpike Road. Continue north on Turnpike Road for about 2.5 miles. Turn right at Upper Turnpike Road. After the turn, the former Smith family home will be immediately on your left.

Notes

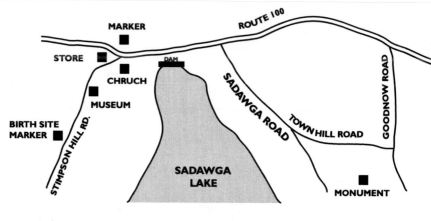

WHITINGHAM

Chapter Ten
Whitingham

Whitingham, with a population close to 1,300, is a quaint village located near Sadawga Lake in southern Vermont, just a few miles north of the Massachusetts border. It was originally called Sadawga Springs, a name probably taken from the Mohawk word meaning "swift water." In 1770, Colonel Whiting and six other British soldiers were given the grant of a township as a reward for their loyalty in the King's service. They named this 36 square mile township Whitingham. On June 1, 1801, Brigham Young was born in this small village.

John Young, his wife Abigail, and their eight children had moved to this area in January 1801. Though John's family originated from Massachusetts, he joined in the land rush to this undeveloped territory. He began farming after purchasing 51 acres of land from his brother-in-law for $100. His ninth child was born just five months later. They named him Brigham after one of his great-grandparents.

PLANNING YOUR TIME

This is a nice rest stop after driving south from Sharon, Vermont and before continuing west to Harmony, Pennsylvania or Palmyra, New York. Allow 30 minutes or more to visit the monument, see the birth site marker, view the lake, and stop at the Whitingham Historical Society Museum. Learning more about Brigham Young at his birth site is a wonderful opportunity.

GETTING THERE

Leaving Sharon, take I-89 south to the White River Junction; take I-91 south towards Brattleboro (about 60 miles). Take exit #2 (Route 9 west exit) towards Brattleboro. After exiting, turn right onto Western Avenue. Western Avenue becomes Marlboro Road, which later becomes Route 9. Continue on Route 9 west, (towards Bennington), for about 11 miles until you bear to the left on Route 100 South to Whitingham. (National Geographic ranked Highway 100 as one of the 10 most scenic highways in America.) Whitingham is about 10 miles further. To see the monument, look for a street sign marked both Goodnow Road and Brigham Young Monument about 7.5 miles after turning onto Route 100. (Watch for the sign, it appears just after rising up a hill and you will need to quickly turn to the left.) The monument is 0.7 miles further after turning left onto Goodnow Road and then turning right onto Town Hill Road. Stop when you see a memorial park on your right and the ball field and monument on your left. To see the state marker and birthplace marker, continue 0.8 miles further on Town Hill Road/Sadawga Road/Route 100. Turn left onto Stimpson Hill Road when you reach the T-shaped intersection with the Brigham Young road sign, church, and store.

Coming from the Palmyra area, head east on I-90 to Albany. Consult your map or previously mentioned map web sites for detailed directions from Albany to Whitingham.

Coming from Harmony/Afton area, take I-88 east to Albany, and consult your maps as mentioned above.

SITES TO SEE

- **Road Sign Indicating the Birthplace of Brigham Young/ Whitingham Village Center** – On the east side of the road, at the intersection of Highway 100 and Stimpson Hill Road, is a sign commemorating Brigham's birth. Also at this intersection are a church and the local country store (which carries Ben and Jerry's ice cream). Though the church and store are old, neither existed during the time the Young family resided here. The road sign, church, store, museum, and birth site marker are all located on what was once the 51 acres owned by John Young.

- **Whitingham Historical Society Museum** – The museum houses exhibits and artifacts of local history including a small display about Brigham Young (notice a pair of eyeglasses and a lock of his hair). Open Sundays only, 2 p.m.–4 p.m., Memorial Day through mid-October. The museum is located in the second building on your left after you turn onto Stimpson Hill Road.

- **Birth Site Marker** – A small marker reading, "Brigham Young, born on this spot 1801, a man of much courage and superb equipment" was placed here sometime before 1900. Though the exact spot of the John Young cabin is not known, this spot is within the boundaries of the 51 acres that he owned. To see the marker, turn on Stimpson Hill Road and go 0.2 miles. The marker will be in front of a home on your right. (Look for it in front of some evergreens.)

Birth Site Marker

Continue just a little further up the hill (also known as Brigham Young Hill) for a beautiful view of Lake Whitingham, also known as the Harriman Reservoir. Over 8 miles long, it is the largest lake entirely within the state of Vermont.

- **Brigham Young Monument** – President George Albert Smith dedicated this 12-foot high granite monument on May 28, 1950. Erected by Brigham's descendants and the Church, it honors the man who was a leader, colonizer, and statesman. The monument is located just off Highway 100 on Town Hill Common (original site of Whitingham Village). It stands at the back of a ballpark (behind centerfield) and across the street from a small memorial park with a pavilion and grassy area. To locate the monument, continue about 1.5 miles southeast from the country store on Highway 100. Shortly after passing the tip of Sadawga Lake, turn right onto Town Hill Road. The Monument and ballpark will be on your right.

Brigham Young Monument

BRIGHAM YOUNG

Brigham Young was born in Whitingham, Vermont on June 1, 1801. He was the 9th of 11 children born to John and Abigail (Nabby) Young. John was rather stern and did not allow his children to laugh or play any musical instruments on Sundays. They did enjoy many other evenings of singing and family gatherings. When Brigham was a young boy, his mother was often sick and so his older sister, Fanny, took care of him. In fact, Brigham would cry if anyone but Fanny tried to hold him. She became adept at holding him on her hip as she did her chores, which even included milking the cows.

Though the family worked hard, there was often not enough money to take care of their basic necessities including food. As a boy, Brigham didn't even own a pair of shoes. Because he always seemed hungry, his family joked that he made a

Brigham Young

path from his bed to the cupboard at night looking for an extra slice of bread. Later, as a father himself, he made sure that his cupboards were always filled with food for his own children to snack on.

One winter, while his father was gone on a three-day trip to buy food, a very hungry Brigham saw a robin perched in a bush. After loading his father's gun, he was able to shoot the bird. Finding less than two spoonfuls of flour at the bottom of the barrel, Brigham cooked the robin and made a stew. The children were so hungry that they ate every morsel.

Growing up, Brigham was a hard worker and spent most of his time working on the family farm. He could also make bread, churn butter, and keep a clean house. At night the family would sit by the fire as their father read from the Bible. Even though Brigham only received about 11 days of formal education during his childhood, he did learn to read. In fact, he valued learning so highly that he became a self-taught, well-educated man who would eventually become a leader, colonizer, writer, and statesman.

Brigham's mother passed away when he was just 14 years old. He would always remember what she had taught: to do those things that were good, not to get angry, and to always honor the name of the Father and Son.

After his mother's death, Brigham Young left home and went to work for a man at his paint store. Always good with his hands, he became a painter, glazier (window maker) and carpenter. His wooden lathe can be seen in the Church History

Museum in Salt Lake City and many pieces of his handiwork such as mantelpieces, stairways, furniture, etc. can also be found in homes and museums.

At the age of 24, Brigham Young married Miriam Works; they would later have two daughters. While living in Mendon, New York, Miriam became very sick with tuberculosis. Each morning, Brigham would take care of his children and Miriam, go to work and return in the evening to prepare dinner, clean the home, tend to Miriam, and put the children to bed.

It was also in Mendon that Brigham first heard of the Book of Mormon. Though many members of his family, including his father, brothers, and sister joined the Church right away, Brigham carefully studied the gospel for two years and was baptized on April 15, 1832. Miriam was baptized about three weeks after Brigham and died just a few months later at the age of 27.

Brigham and his close friend Heber C. Kimball traveled to Kirtland, Ohio where the Prophet was living. From the moment of their first meeting, Brigham remained a true and loyal friend to Joseph. Brigham served with the Prophet in Zion's Camp and was President of the Twelve Apostles at the time Joseph was martyred in Carthage on June 27, 1844.

Under Brigham's leadership, the Saints in Nauvoo continued working on the Nauvoo Temple while preparing for their trek out West. During the long journey across the plains, Brigham was the first to rise and the last to retire. Though extremely hard working and steadfast in following the principles of the Gospel, he also possessed a hearty laugh and encouraged singing and dancing around the campfires at night.

Brigham Young was the prophet and leader of the Church for almost 30 years. During this period, the Salt Lake Temple was under construction, the city grew and flourished, and hundreds of other settlements in the western United States, Canada, and Mexico were formed. Throughout his life, Brigham was dedicated to the Lord and humbly credited all that he was able to accomplish to Him.

Brigham Young died on August 29, 1877 at the age of 76. The last words he uttered before his death were: "Joseph, Joseph, Joseph." Brigham Young had been a carpenter, missionary, husband, father, apostle, pioneer, governor, prophet and president of the Church. A statue honoring this prophet stands in the Capitol Rotunda in Washington D.C.

Notes

Notes

Notes

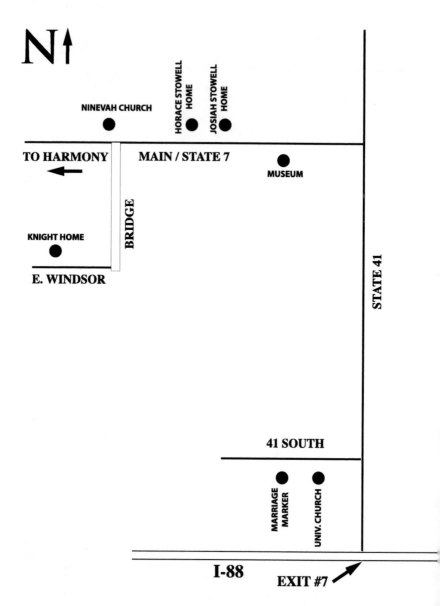

South Bainbridge
(Afton) and Colesville

New York & Pennsylvania

Chapter Eleven
South Bainbridge (Afton) and Colesville

South Bainbridge, now called Afton, is located about 30 miles northeast of Binghamton in southern New York. Though the area has changed names several times, it was known as South Bainbridge at the time Joseph and Emma came here to be married. Prior to their marriage, Joseph lived and worked on a local farm owned by Josiah Stowell. The Prophet also experienced his first arrest, trial, and subsequent acquittal in South Bainbridge.

The Township of Colesville is located about 7 miles southwest of Afton. Many significant early Church events also took place here: the organization of the first branch of the Church in 1830, numerous baptisms at the Knight farm (including Emma Smith), the first latter-day miracle, and another arrest, trial, and acquittal of the Prophet.

PLANNING YOUR TIME

If time is short, take 5 minutes to exit the freeway and drive to the front gates of the Afton Fairgrounds to see the marker. We suggest you take 30-60 minutes to drive through South Bainbridge (Afton) and nearby Colesville (Nineveh) to see several Church historical homes and sites, including the homes of Josiah Stowell and Joseph Knight. All are less than 10 miles from the freeway.

GETTING THERE

Traveling on I-88, take the Afton Exit #7, which puts you onto State 41. After exiting, make a left turn onto 41 S. The fairgrounds are about 0.2 miles further on your left. To visit the museum, stay on State 41 and go straight into Afton (0.7 miles from the freeway exit). Turn left onto Main Street, which is also State 7, and the museum will be on your left. To drive by the Josiah Stowell home, go past the museum and continue on State 7 for about 4 miles.

To drive by the Knight home and the general area of early baptisms, turn off of State 7 just before the Nineveh Presbyterian Church. Take the bridge over the Susquehanna River and then make a right turn onto East Windsor. The sites will be a little further on both sides of the road.

To continue on to Harmony, go back across the Susquehanna River and turn left onto State 7. Continue on State 7 and make a left turn at the I-88/E 79 markers. This will take you into Harmony (see more detailed directions in Harmony chapter).

SIGNIFICANT EVENTS

*   **Joseph appeared in court at South Bainbridge on March 20, 1826.** – According to the Prophet's own account, Josiah Stowell, having heard about a Spanish silver mine, hired Joseph "to dig for the silver mine, at which I continued to work for nearly a month, without success in our undertaking, and finally I prevailed with the old gentleman to cease digging after it. Hence arose the very prevalent story of my having been a money-digger" (HC 1:17). Josiah next hired Joseph to work on his nearby farm. Joseph's search for buried treasure

resulted in a misdemeanor charge against him for being a "disorderly person." Though the Prophet was acquitted of the charges, this would be the first of many times that he would be arrested on false charges.

- **Joseph and Emma were married here in January 1827** – Joseph had met and had fallen in love with Emma while boarding at the Hale home in Harmony, Pennsylvania. During the two years that he lived and worked in the area, Joseph asked Isaac Hale on two different occasions for permission to marry his daughter. Both times Mr. Hale refused to give his consent. In a discussion with his mother, Joseph commented to her that, "he had come to the conclusion of getting married if we had no objections." Joseph's choice of wife was, "Miss Emma Hale, a young lady whom he had been extremely fond of since his first introduction to her" (HJS pg. 126). Joseph's parents not only gave their blessing but encouraged him to bring Emma back to their home to live with the family.

Photograph courtesy of Charles Decker

Squire Tarbell Home

On January 18, 1827, Joseph and Emma eloped to South Bainbridge, because "owing to my continuing to assert that I had seen a vision, persecution still followed me, and my wife's father's family were very much opposed to our being married" (HC 1:17). They were married at the home of Squire Tarbell and returned to Manchester, New York, to live with the Smith family in their frame home until December of that same year. Joseph was 21 years old and Emma was 22.

- **The Prophet was again brought to trial in South Bainbridge in 1830** – While Joseph was in the nearby town of Colesville, he was arrested "on the charge of being a disorderly person, of setting the country in an uproar by preaching the Book of Mormon, etc." (HC 1:88). The trial took place in South Bainbridge on July 1, 1830, a little over four years after Joseph's first arrest here. Joseph Knight hired two attorneys to defend the Prophet. Josiah Stowell, two daughters of Josiah, and several others were questioned and testified concerning Joseph's character. Although he was found innocent, Joseph was rearrested almost immediately on similar charges in Broome County. The Prophet was represented by the same two attorneys from his previous trial, and again, this time at Colesville in Broome County, he was found innocent.

- **Joseph Knight Sr. and Family** – Joseph Knight first met Joseph Smith when he hired him to work on his farm in 1826. Considering young Joseph to be one of the best workers he ever had, Joseph Knight let Joseph take his horse and sleigh to visit Emma Hale in Harmony, Pennsylvania. On the evening of September 22, 1827, Joseph borrowed Brother Knight's horse and wagon for the three-mile drive from the frame home to the Hill Cumorah, where Joseph was entrusted with the gold plates. Joseph Knight visited the young couple at their home in Harmony in the spring of 1829, bringing needed gifts of food, money, and writing materials. Soon after the Church was organized on April 6, 1830, Joseph visited the Knight family and found the family "friendly and hospitable" as usual (HC 1:81). During this visit, Joseph held meetings to teach and discuss gospel principles. After one such meeting, Newel Knight (Joseph Knight's son), went out into the woods to pray but was overcome by an evil spirit. The Prophet recorded that the rebuking of this spirit was "the first miracle which was done in the Church...but it was done by God" (HC 1:83). Despite strong opposition, thirteen people were baptized at the Knight farm on June 28, 1830, including Emma Smith, Joseph Knight Sr. and his wife Polly, and Joseph Knight Jr. (HC 1:88). The Knight family remained active members of the Church. Though Polly Knight was very ill while living in Kirtland, she refused to be left behind when the Colesville Branch moved to Missouri. Her greatest wish was to set foot in Zion. Polly died less than two weeks after her arrival in Independence. The Prophet attended her funeral and later recorded, "This was the first death in the Church in this land, and I can say a worthy member sleeps in Jesus till the resurrection" (HC 1:199). Joseph Knight Sr. died on February 3, 1847 in Mt. Pisgah, Iowa while en route to the Salt Lake Valley.

- **Colesville Branch** – Many of the early converts from this area were baptized at the Knight farm. The Colesville Branch was organized in October 1830 and soon grew to almost 70 committed members of the Church. Under the leadership of Newel Knight, they left their homes in the spring of 1831 for Kirtland, Ohio. The Colesville Branch lived briefly in Kirtland before continuing on to Jackson County, Missouri. They became the first branch of the Church located in the Independence area.

SITES TO SEE

Credit for the location of many of these sites goes to Charles Decker. He is a fifth generation Afton resident and local historian. We express thanks to Charles for his knowledge and for the time spent in helping us locate these sites.

- **Universalist Church** – After exiting the freeway and turning left on River Road, you will pass a brown church (about the fourth building on your left) just before arriving at the fairgrounds. Tradition says (and Charles Decker agrees) that the Knight family once worshipped at this church. According to the Prophet, "Mr. Knight and his family were Universalists, but were willing to reason with me upon my religious views" (HC 1:81). ***Update – the building was just demolished in June 2009.**

- **Marker at the site of Joseph and Emma's marriage** – Joseph and Emma were married in the home of Zachariah Tarbell, Justice of the Peace. Though the home is no longer standing, the blue and yellow New York sign placed here around 1935 reads: "Mormon House. Joseph Smith, founder of the Mormon Church, was

Marriage Marker

married in this house Jan. 18, 1827 to Emily Hale." Notice that the sign says "Emily," not Emma. Squire Tarbell was not a Mormon, but the term "Mormon House" is applied to the home because of Joseph and Emma's marriage. You will find the marker on the left side of the road, just past the entrance to the Afton fairgrounds.

• **Afton Inn** – The inn which is located on your right, just before reaching the museum, is possibly the site where Joseph stood trial in 1826 and was acquitted of being a "disorderly person" (HC 1:88-89).

• **Afton Historical Society** – The Afton Historical Society has a small museum containing several items of interest including a Civil War medical kit. It contains instruments similar to those used by surgeons performing leg surgery in 1813 on seven year-old Joseph Smith Jr. Also notice one of the original mantle pieces from the Zachariah Tarbell home. On the mantle sits a bust of the Prophet and above the mantle hangs a painting of the Tarbell home. (Charles Decker donated the mantle piece to the museum; a second piece is in his home.) Don't leave without taking a picture of a historical marker that once marked a spot "up the creek" where some claimed that Joseph dug and found some of the gold plates. (Which was of course not true.) The museum is open Sunday afternoons from 2 p.m. to 4 p.m. from Memorial Day through Labor Day, or by calling Charles Decker at 607-639-2720 to schedule an appointment. It is located .3 miles from the stop sign, at 116 Main Street.

• **Schoolhouse** – Josiah Stowell Jr. and Joseph Smith became friends and schoolmates when the Prophet worked for Josiah Sr. from 1825 to 1827. Josiah Jr. was the youngest child of Josiah Sr. and was about 16 years old when 19 year old Joseph first came to work on the Stowell farm. In a letter written by Josiah Stowell Jr. to John Fullmer on February 17, 1843, Josiah Jr. stated that he attended school with Joseph Smith during one winter (letter in LDS Church Archives). The schoolhouse that Joseph briefly attended burned down around 1891. The building now located at 439 State 7 stands in the general area where the schoolhouse once stood. It is just west of the Afton Museum (about 4 miles from the exit and about 0.6 miles before the Stowell home). It is privately owned and not available for tours.

- **Josiah Stowell Sr. Home and Farm Site** – Records indicate that this two-story white home is the original 1810 frame home of Josiah Stowell. Joseph was employed by Josiah, briefly helping him look for a Spanish silver mine and later working on his farm. Joseph was working for Josiah on this farm at the time he married Emma (HC 1:17). Josiah became a member of the Church and attended

Josiah Stowell Home

the Colesville Branch. Both he and Joseph Knight were at the Smith frame home when Joseph returned with the gold plates on September 22, 1827 (HJS p. 137). Josiah stayed in New York and did not go with the Saints to Missouri. He later moved from South Bainbridge and purchased land in Tioga County, New York. In a letter written to the Prophet on December 19, 1843, Josiah wrote of his desire to come to Nauvoo (letter in LDS Church Archives). Brother Stowell was ill at the time but hoped to be well enough to travel the following spring. Unfortunately, Josiah was never able to join the Saints in Nauvoo. He died in New York on May 12, 1844 at the age of 76. The Josiah Stowell home is located at 323 State 7 (4 miles from the stop sign). The home will be on your right, next to Reilings Garage. The home is owned by members of the Church and permission is given to walk the grounds. Please park in the driveway and be careful not to block the neighbor's business.

- **Horace Stowell Home** – The blue home, to the left of the Josiah Stowell home, was once the home of Josiah's son, Horace Stowell. Notice the plaque on the home which indicates it was built in 1824. The home is privately owned and not available for tours.

- **Nineveh Presbyterian Church** – Though it is not the original church, many of the converts of the Colesville Branch previously belonged to this faith. The two-story white home located just to the right of the church probably incorporates some of the original church structure. Both the church and home are located west of the Stowell home and about 6.3 miles from the freeway exit.

Joseph Knight Home

- **Joseph Knight Home** – Local records indicate that this is the former home of Joseph Knight Sr. He was a good and life-long friend of the Prophet Joseph Smith. The pond where many of the previously mentioned baptisms occurred was probably located across the street from this home and situated back towards the hills. A member of the Church owns the home and has given permission to walk the grounds. To find this home, turn off of State 7 just before the Nineveh Presbyterian Church. Take the bridge over the Susquehanna River and then make a right turn onto East Windsor. Continue .5 miles and you will see the home on your right at 1963 East Windsor Road.

RESTAURANTS

- **Ninevah General Store** – This small store sells gas, groceries, misc. supplies, and it has a small deli featuring sandwiches, calzones, pizza, salads, ice cream, and breakfast items. Located at 3017 Route 7. 607-693-1313

Several local diners located on Main Street include Afton Grill & Bakery, Vincent's Italian Restaurant, and Henry's.

LODGING

Afton does not have any lodging options. However, you will find lodgings nearby at Bainbridge, Sidney (12 miles to the east), Oneonta (30 miles to the east), and Binghamton (25 miles to the west).

Notes

_____

_____

_____

_____

_____

_____

_____

_____

_____

_____

_____

_____

_____

_____

_____

_____

Notes

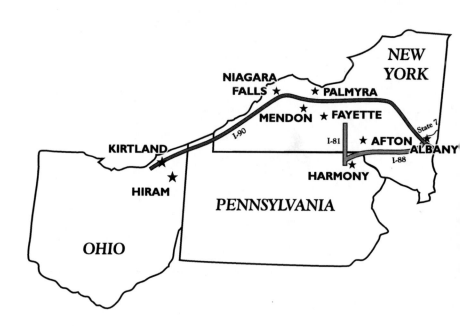

Chapter Twelve
Harmony
(Oakland)

Harmony Township, now called Oakland Township, is located in the northeastern part of Pennsylvania, very close to the New York State line. Isaac and Elizabeth Hale were some of the first permanent settlers in this area. They moved from Vermont in 1791 along with Elizabeth's brother and his wife. Isaac and Elizabeth raised their nine children in a home located near the banks of the Susquehanna River; their seventh child was a daughter named Emma. In 1825, Joseph Smith Jr. and his father boarded with the Hale family for about a month while working at a local mining operation. Joseph met and fell in love with Emma. They were married on January 18, 1827 (see South Bainbridge chapter). Joseph and Emma moved back to Harmony in December of 1827, first living with the Hale family and then moving nearby to a small farm.

Many significant events in Church history occurred in this area from 1828 to 1830. Most of the Book of Mormon was translated in Harmony, including the first 116 pages that Martin Harris was allowed to borrow and subsequently had stolen. It was in this area that Joseph Smith and Oliver Cowdery received the Aaronic Priesthood from John the Baptist. The Prophet also received fifteen revelations now found in D&C 3-13, 24-27. Sadly, it was also here that Emma and Joseph lost their first child, Alvin, who was born and died on the same day.

PLANNING YOUR TIME

This is a wonderful and important stop to make while traveling through the area or as a day trip from Palmyra. Harmony is located about 150 miles southeast of the Manchester/Palmyra area. While there, allow yourself about 30-60 minutes to view Joseph and Emma's home site, the home site of her parents, the cemetery where Joseph and Emma's first child and other extended family members are buried, and to see the Monument to the Aaronic Priesthood. Three of the sites are next to each other and the other is located across the street. There is plenty of parking, a grassy area to stretch your legs, but no restroom facilities.

GETTING THERE

Traveling on I-88, take the Nineveh exit #6. Turn towards Harpursville and follow State 79 E. under the freeway. (You will see a gas station/convenience store on your left.) The distance from the exit to the monument is about 25 miles (about a 30 minute drive). With the Susquehanna River on your left, stay on State 79 which becomes State (Penn.) 92 at the state line. Continue south on State 92. After traveling 22 miles you will pass a bridge (on your left but don't cross) that leads into the town of Susquehanna. The road that crosses the bridge is State 92, but the road continuing on becomes River Street 171 North. After passing the bridge, continue about 1.5 miles on State 171 North and you will see the McKune Cemetery and Aaronic Priesthood Restoration Monument on your left. After visiting the sites, continue on State 171 for 6.5 miles further and you will reach the junction of I-81 and State 171.

Coming from Nineveh via Afton on State 7, turn left at the I-88/E 79 markers (located 2 miles from the bridge). Continue on 79 (going under the overpass) and follow the previous directions.

If you are traveling on I-81, take the Hallstead/Great Bend exit. Take State 171 heading east and you will see the Priesthood Restoration Monument on your right, about 6.5 miles further.

SITES TO SEE

- **Joseph and Emma Smith Home Site** – The couple's home once stood just to the right of the present Aaronic Priesthood Monument. The Prophet purchased this 13 1/2-acre parcel of land from Isaac Hale and also a two-story frame home from Jesse Hale, Emma's brother. Joseph then had the frame home moved onto his parcel of land. While living in this home, Joseph translated much of the Book of Mormon with the help of several scribes.

Photograph courtesy of Charles Decker

Joseph and Emma Smith Home
(Center section of home is the original)

including Martin Harris, Emma, her brother Reuben Hale, and Joseph's brother Samuel Smith. The largest part was translated with the help of Oliver Cowdery. On June 15, 1828, Joseph and Emma's first child, Alvin, was born but died shortly after birth. Emma also nearly died and Joseph spent several weeks lovingly nursing her back to health while anxiously waiting for Martin Harris to return with the 116 pages of manuscript. After moving to Fayette to finish the translation in June of 1829, Joseph returned to his home at Harmony around August of that same year. With persecution increasing, and with concerns for their own safety, Joseph and Emma permanently left Harmony in late August of 1830, moving first to Fayette and ultimately on to Ohio. Joseph arranged for the sale of his Harmony property while he was living in Kirtland. The home was destroyed by fire in 1919.

- **Aaronic Priesthood Monument** – Dr. Avard Fairbanks sculpted this beautiful granite monument that was dedicated on June 18, 1960. The three bronze figures on the monument depict John the Baptist conferring the Aaronic Priesthood upon Joseph Smith and Oliver Cowdery. Take time to read the inscription at the base of the monument and also read the information on the Aaronic Priesthood Restoration sign immediately to the right of the monument.

- **McKune Cemetery** – This small cemetery is located just to the left of the Aaronic Priesthood Monument. With your back to the monument, the graves of Isaac and Elizabeth Hale are located about the sixth row from the far left corner (very close to the road). Notice that the original headstones are imbedded in new headstones so that you can view the original on one side and you are able to

McKune Cemetery

read the text on the other side. Isaac passed away in 1839 at the age of 75 and Elizabeth died 3 years later also at age 75. About four headstones to the right of Elizabeth Hale's grave is the grave of Alvin Smith, who was born and died on June 15, 1828. Also notice the gravestone just to the right of Alvin's. It is that of his cousin, Nancy Hale, the daughter of Jesse and Mary Hale (Emma's brother and sister-in-law). Nancy died just a few months before Alvin, on January 29, 1828. She was just 2 1/2 years old.

- **Isaac and Elizabeth Hale Home Site** –The Prophet first met Emma while boarding in this home. Isaac did not approve of Joseph's interest in his daughter. Considering Joseph uneducated and of dubious character, Isaac thought his cultured, schoolteacher daughter could do better. Less than a year after their marriage, Joseph and Emma temporarily lived with the Hales before moving into their own two-story frame home. Joseph was threatened by mobs while working on the translation but Isaac had become more favorable towards his son-in-law and used his influence to keep the mobs at bay (JS–H 1:75). However Isaac's feelings were again turned against the Prophet by the time Joseph and Emma returned to Harmony from Fayette. A minister had told many falsehoods about the Prophet, and Isaac believed them. Without Isaac's support, the persecution escalated, finally forcing Joseph and Emma to leave permanently. The Hale home site is located across the street from the other sites. The original home burned down in the 1870s and was rebuilt in the 1880s. The rebuilt home was eventually torn down in the early 1950s. To view the home site, walk across State 171 from the Aaronic Priesthood Monument (be very careful crossing – cars come by very fast). Almost directly across the street from the red wooden Aaronic Priesthood sign, you will see a trail that leads you on a short walk across a small stream bed and into a meadow. Turn left at the meadow and look near the road for a split-rail fence enclosure with a sign identifying the home site area (not the first rail enclosure but the second one).

Isaac Hale Home Site

- **Susquehanna River** – Many important events occurred in and along the banks of the Susquehanna River, although their exact locations were not recorded. While Joseph and Oliver Cowdery were translating 3rd Nephi, they were impressed with the importance of baptism. On May 15, 1829, Joseph and Oliver went into the woods and prayed near the banks of the river. As they were praying, "a messenger from heaven descended in a cloud of light" (JS-H 1:68). The messenger was John the Baptist, who baptized Christ (Matthew 3:13). John the Baptist laid his hands upon the heads of Joseph and Oliver, conferring the Aaronic Priesthood. Following John's instructions, Joseph then baptized Oliver, after which Oliver baptized Joseph. (For a more detailed account read JS-H 1:68-74.) It was also "in the wilderness between Harmony, Susquehanna county, and Colesville, Broome county, on the Susquehanna river" that Joseph and Oliver received the Melchizedek Priesthood from Peter, James, and John (D&C 128:20).

Susquehanna River

PHOTO SPOTS

- **Susquehanna River** – Just two miles south of the monument is a bridge which spans the river and takes you directly into the small town of Susquehanna. Walk halfway across this bridge for a great picture of the Susquehanna River.

RESTAURANTS/LODGING

Several small diners are located in the town of Susquehanna. You will find a larger selection of fast food choices west of Harmony, located just off of I-81 at the Great Bend/Halstead exit. (We usually stop at Subway.)

* If you are continuing from Harmony to Fayette and Palmyra via NY 81, notice the rest area/tourism center just 4 miles from the entrance of 81. Inside you will find nice restrooms, helpful staff with maps and travel guides, and vending machines. This is also a great stop for a wonderful view of the surrounding area.

Notes

Notes

_____

_____

_____

_____

_____

_____

_____

_____

_____

_____

_____

_____

_____

_____

_____

_____

Notes

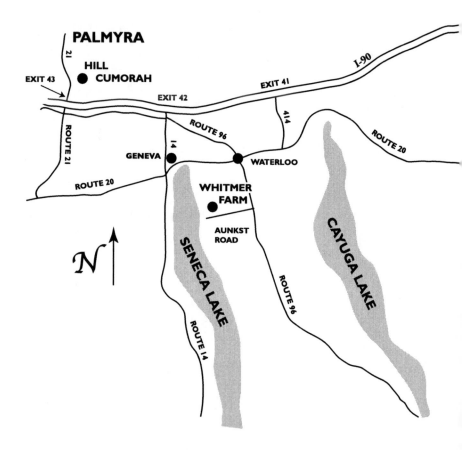

Chapter Thirteen
Fayette

The Township of Fayette is located southeast of Palmyra in Seneca County, nestled between the Seneca and Cayuga Lakes. First named Washington, the town was renamed on April 6, 1808 after General LaFayette, a hero in the Revolutionary War. Just twenty-two years later, also on April 6, the Church of Jesus Christ was officially organized here in a small log home owned by Peter Whitmer Sr.

Peter Whitmer Sr. and his wife Mary moved their family from Harrisburg, Pennsylvania to Fayette in 1809. By 1819, their farm encompassed about 100 acres of land covered with dense hardwood trees. After a considerable amount of clearing, the family built their 20' by 30' log cabin. It would be home for the couple and their seven children: Christian, Jacob, John, David, Catherine (who would marry Hiram Page), Peter Jr., and Elizabeth Ann (who would marry Oliver Cowdery). David and Oliver would later become two of the Three Witnesses to the Book of Mormon; while Christian, Jacob, John, Peter Jr., and Hiram Page would be five of the Eight Witnesses.

In the early years of the Church, from 1829 to 1831, many significant and spiritual events took place on or near this farm. Being able to visit the rebuilt log home and learn more about this special site is a wonderful opportunity you don't want to miss.

PLANNING YOUR TIME

The Peter Whitmer farm is a "must see" stop while visiting the Palmyra area. The drive from Palmyra to the farm is about 45 minutes. Allow an additional 45 minutes for the tour of the Peter Whitmer home and visitors' center.

GETTING THERE

The Peter Whitmer Farm is located just a few miles south of Waterloo and about 27 miles southeast of Palmyra. Coming from Palmyra on Route 21 South, turn left onto Route 96. (Watch for Route 96 and Whitmer farm marker just after the "Welcome to the Village of Waterloo" sign.) After going through Waterloo on 96, look for the Whitmer Farm signs indicating a right turn onto Aunkst Road.

Traveling on I-90, take exit 42 or exit 41, heading south. Follow the signs to Waterloo and continue south on 96. After passing through Waterloo, watch for the Peter Whitmer Farm signs.

Going from Harmony to Fayette (110 miles or 2 1/2 hour drive), take I-81 N. for 31 miles. Take exit #8 (Ithaca) and turn right. Continue about .8 miles and turn left at the stop sign (towards Ithaca) onto Route 79. Continue another 31 miles on Route 79 and turn onto Route 96 for 38 miles. (You will be going through Ithaca – follow the signs for 96 North.) Stay on Route 96 and watch for Church signage indicating a left turn on Aunkst Road. After making the turn on Aunkst, go about 1 mile to the Peter Whitmer Farm.

SIGNIFICANT EVENTS

In June 1829, the Prophet Joseph Smith and Oliver Cowdery left Harmony, Pennsylvania and arrived at the Whitmer farm. (Emma followed at a later date.) Many significant and marvelous events occurred during their stay: the translation of the Book of Mormon was completed, the Three Witnesses were allowed to see the gold plates, Mary Whitmer was also shown the gold plates, the Church was officially organized, twenty revelations were received, and many new converts were baptized.

Peter Whitmer Log Home

- **The Three Witnesses are shown the gold plates** – While translating, Joseph and Oliver Cowdery (acting as scribe) learned that three special witnesses would be chosen. Oliver, David Whitmer, and Martin Harris sincerely desired to be chosen and so Joseph inquired of the Lord. In response, the Prophet received the revelation recorded in D&C 17 which declared that through their faith, the three men could indeed see the plates and other sacred items. In June of 1829, Joseph and the Three Witnesses retired to a secluded spot near the Whitmer home where they were privileged to see the plates, shown to them by angel Moroni (see HC 1:52-57 for a detailed account). Their written testimony of this event can be read at the beginning of the Book of Mormon.

- **Translation is completed** - Though most of the translation was done in Harmony, Joseph completed translating the gold plates at the Whitmer home around late June/early July of 1829.

- **Mary Whitmer views the gold plates** – Another special person given the privilege of seeing the plates was Mary Whitmer. Somewhat overwhelmed by the extra work in taking care of her houseguests, she was shown the plates by a heavenly being (probably Moroni) as she was going out to the barn to milk the cows (CHC 1:127).

- **The Church is organized on April 6, 1830** – As directed by revelation, the Church was organized on this date in the Whitmer home (D&C 20). Although about 50 people filled the two rooms and witnessed the event, only Joseph and five others formally participated in the organization, thus complying with the state's legal requirements. The participants were: Joseph, Oliver Cowdery, Hyrum Smith, Samuel Smith, David Whitmer, and Peter Whitmer Jr. The meeting began with a prayer followed by a unanimous vote taken to "proceed and be organized as a Church according to said commandment which we had received" (HC 1:77). During this meeting, Joseph and Oliver were ordained as elders and the sacrament was administered. It was also during this spiritual occasion that Joseph received the revelation now recorded as D&C 21 in which he was called to be a seer and prophet. Several of those who witnessed the sacred events desired to be baptized that day including the Prophet's father, Martin Harris, and Porter Rockwell (HC 1:79). (Lucy Smith was also baptized on this same day or shortly after.)

- **Headquarters of the Church** – After the Church was organized on April 6, 1830, the Whitmer home became the headquarters of the Church until early January of 1831, when Joseph and Emma relocated as commanded "to the Ohio." The Whitmer family soon followed the Prophet, as did most of the other members of the Church.

- **Revelations received here** – Joseph received twenty revelations while living in Fayette. They are recorded in D&C 14-18, 20, 21, and 28 – 40.

- **First three conferences held here** – A little over two months after the Church was organized, the first general conference of the Church was held in the Whitmer home on June 9, 1830. Twelve people were baptized after this conference including two of the Prophet's brothers, William and Don Carlos, and his sister, Katherine. The second conference was held about three months later, September 26 – 28. The third and final conference held in Fayette was on January 2, 1831. It was during this conference that Joseph received a revelation containing a second call for the Saints to "go to the Ohio" (D&C 38:32).

- **Converts baptized in this area** – Though we do not know the exact location, many early members were baptized in Seneca Lake. They included: Hyrum Smith, Peter Whitmer Jr., David Whitmer, Hiram Page, William Smith, Don Carlos Smith, Katherine Smith, and other members of the Whitmer family (HC 1:51, 81, and 86).

SITES TO SEE

- **Peter Whitmer Visitors' Center** – Free guided tours begin at the visitors' center located in the west wing of the church. Learn about the important events that occurred in and around this area and enjoy the numerous paintings depicting the organization of the Church. Before leaving, pick up a free handout entitled, *Significant Events at the Peter Whitmer Farm*. Restrooms are located here. Open Monday thru Saturday 9 a.m.–7 p.m. in summer (but closes at 6 p.m. in spring/fall, and is open from 12:30 p.m.–5 p.m. in winter) and Sunday 12:30 p.m.–7 p.m. in summer (12:30 p.m.–5 p.m. in winter, 12:30 p.m. – 6 p.m. in spring and fall). Call to verify current hours. The visitors' center is located at 1451 Aunkst Road. 315-539-2552

Whitmer Kitchen

Upstairs Bedroom

- **Peter Whitmer Farm** – The Whitmer log home was reconstructed on the original site and dedicated by President Spencer W. Kimball during general conference on April 6, 1980. This date marked the 150th anniversary of the organization of the Church.

LDS CHURCH SERVICES

An 1830 colonial-style church and visitors' center is located next to the Peter Whitmer home. The Fayette Ward Sacrament Meeting begins at 9:30 a.m.

ATM

There is an ATM machine located inside Connie's Diner; several banks are located on Main Street in Waterloo.

ACTIVITIES/SHOPPING

Contact the Seneca tourism department at 315-568-2906 or www.senecachamber.org to receive a free tourism packet. Waterloo is known as the "Birthplace of Memorial Day," while Seneca Falls is the "Birthplace of Women's Rights." (The Joseph Smith Sr. family first moved to Waterloo, after leaving their Manchester farm, before moving on to Ohio.)

- **Seneca Lake State Park** – Enjoy a family swim at Seneca Lake where many early Church baptisms occurred. The park features picnic areas, large beach area with lifeguards on duty during summer season, marina, bathhouse, restrooms, playground, and a fun waterpark playground (geared for children up to age 14). Open sunrise to sunset year-round, but services are open and fee of $7/per car charged from May thru Oct. Located about 15 miles west of Fayette at Routes 5 and 20 in nearby Geneva. 315-789-2331.

- **Waterloo Premium Outlets** – Over 2.5 million shoppers annually visit this discount mall featuring over 100 stores including Polo, Gap, Liz Claiborne, Nautica, and Oshkosh. Fast food options include Arby's, Burger King, Subway, and Villa Pizza. Traveling on I-90, take exit 42 and turn onto Route 318 heading east. The outlets are located about 3 miles further at 655 Route 318, Waterloo. 315-539-1100.

RESTAURANTS

The closest dining choices are in nearby Waterloo. Local favorites include:

- **Connie's Diner** – Enjoy breakfast, lunch, or dinner at an affordable price. Located at 205 E. Main Street. 315-539-9556.

- **The First Dragon** – This Chinese restaurant is located at the intersection of Routes 96/5/20. 315-539-8882.

- **Abigail's** – Family-owned fine dining restaurant serving lunch and dinner. Located east of Waterloo at Routes 5 and 20. 315-539-9300.

- **Fast food options** along Main Street include Pizza Hut and Subway. There are many other choices on Route 414 located just east of Waterloo. Choices include McDonald's, KFC, and Taco Bell.

- **Belhurst Castle** – Overlooking Seneca Lake, the 1880s Belhurst Castle offers both lodging and fine dining. Very popular is the Sunday brunch served from 11 a.m.–1:45 pm. Daily breakfast, lunch, and dinner options also available. Located in Geneva at 4069 Route 14 South. 315-781-0201.

LODGING

- **Holiday Inn** – Featuring 148 rooms and on-site restaurant. Located at 2468 Route 414 in Waterloo. 315-539-5011 or 800-465-4329.

- **Microtel** – This inn has 69 rooms. Located just east of Waterloo in Seneca Falls at 1966 Route 5 & 20. 800-771-7171 or 315-539-8438.

- **Ramada Inn** – Featuring 148 rooms and on-site restaurant, fitness center and indoor swimming pool. Located about 5 miles west of Waterloo at 41 Lakefront Drive, Geneva. 315-789-0400

CAMPING

- See Palmyra chapter (camping) for local choices.

Notes

Notes

_____

_____

_____

_____

_____

_____

_____

_____

_____

_____

_____

_____

_____

_____

_____

_____

_____

_____

Notes

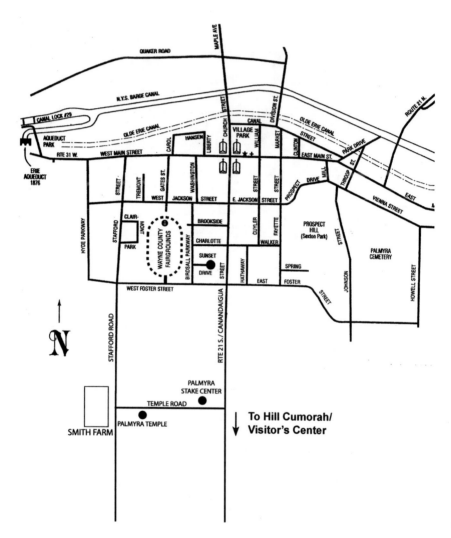

Village of Palmyra

Courtesy of Canaltown Days Committee

Chapter Fourteen
Palmyra

The Village of Palmyra is located about 28 miles southeast of Rochester on the western side of New York State. In the late 1700s, this area became a desired destination for settlers looking for fertile farmland to grow crops and to raise a family. The nearby lakes and densely wooded forests provided the water and lumber necessary to begin a new life in this undeveloped territory. Both the village and township went through a series of name changes until 1798 when they were named "Palmyra," after an ancient city in Syria. This city had been built around a desert oasis near an important trade route used by the Roman and Persian empires. Like its namesake, modern Palmyra also became an important village near the waters of a flourishing trade route upon completion of the Erie Canal in 1825. Many citizens of Palmyra prospered during the Canal Period of 1822 to 1853. Several homes built during this period still stand today, silent reminders of a storied past.

For Latter-day Saints, visiting the Palmyra/Manchester area provides a tangible reminder of a very special and sacred time in early Church history. A small rebuilt log cabin beside a grove of trees reminds us of one of the most significant events that has occurred since the resurrection of Jesus Christ. The nearby frame home evokes stories of joyful moments, harrowing escapes, and personal hardships. To the east stands a wooded "drumlin" or hill with the Angel Moroni Monument atop. It was on this hillside that the angel Moroni delivered the gold plates, containing a record of the history of his people, to a young man named Joseph Smith. A home site reminds us of one individual's personal sacrifice in offering his farm as payment for the printing of this translated record. A tour inside a restored red brick building will explain the process used to print the Book of Mormon, the culminating gift we enjoy today because of those many early sacrifices.

PLANNING YOUR TIME

To really experience Palmyra, allow at least two days to visit the "must see" sites in this area. They include the Hill Cumorah and visitors' center, the Sacred Grove, the Smith log house, the Smith frame house, Book of Mormon publishing site, and the Peter Whitmer farm in nearby Fayette. (To do it all in a day is a very rushed experience.) "Nice to see" stops include the Swift Cemetery, Martin Harris home site, and Lock #29 on the Erie Canal. If time allows, try to include some of the other local museums, sights, and activities, or take a day trip to Niagara Falls (just 90 minutes away). For those planning to attend the Palmyra Temple – be sure to call ahead and schedule your session at 315-597-6001. To receive a free tourism packet on Palmyra, call 315-597-5521 or visit the Palmyra web site at www.palmyrany.com. For additional information on area attractions, call Wayne County tourism at 800-527-6510 or the Rochester tourism department at 800-677-7282. You can also stop at the Palmyra Information Center inside the Palmyra Town Hall located at 1180 Canandaigua Road. (This building was a former LDS stake center.)

GETTING THERE

Traveling on I-90, take exit #43 and turn north onto Route 21. The Hill Cumorah Visitors' Center is about 3 miles further. (I-90 in New York State is a toll road.)

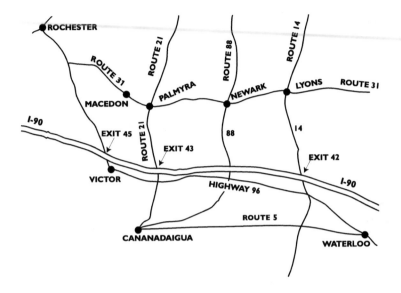

For some of us, the concepts of villages, towns, townships, and counties may be somewhat confusing. Cities, villages (incorporated), and hamlets (unincorporated), are located within towns. Towns, sometimes referred to as townships, make up each county. This will help you understand why the Village of Manchester is located south of I-90, while the Joseph Smith farm and Hill Cumorah lie north of I-90 in the Town of Manchester in Ontario County. Just two miles further north of the Smith farm is the Village of Palmyra in Wayne County. After this explanation, you will hopefully understand why we have listed all the "sites to see" without differentiating between village, township, or county. It simplifies directions, as they are all located in close proximity to each other. Further simplifying directions, we will often refer to the junction of Canandaigua Street (Route 21) and Main Street (Route 31), in the village of Palmyra, as the "Main intersection." (The "locals" call this corner "the four churches.")

SIGNIFICANT EVENTS

Many marvelous events occurred in this area from 1816 to 1830. Fourteen-year-old Joseph Smith saw and talked with God the Father and His Son, Jesus Christ, in the Sacred Grove in 1820. Just three years later, Joseph first saw the gold plates, shown to him by the angel Moroni at the Hill Cumorah. After four years of preparation and training, the Prophet was finally allowed to take the plates and begin translating them. Due to escalating persecution, Joseph and his new bride Emma were soon forced to relocate to Harmony, Pennsylvania in December of 1827. Despite those who tried to thwart the work, the translation of the plates was completed and the Prophet made arrangements for the first 5,000 copies of the Book of Mormon to be published in August of 1829. Upon completion of the first printing in March of 1830, the spreading of the Gospel began in earnest. Early converts included Joseph Knight of Colesville, Brigham Young and Heber C. Kimball of Mendon, and George A. Smith of St. Lawrence County, New York. On April 6, 1830, the Church was officially organized in nearby Fayette. Several were baptized that day including the Prophet's father. But as membership in the restored Church increased, so did the persecution. At the third and final conference in New York, the Prophet received the second revelation calling for the Saints to go to Ohio. Joseph and Emma left in February of 1831, with other members of the Church following shortly after.

To better understand and appreciate the significance of Palmyra, read through the list of suggested sites to visit. Walking through the homes, hearing the stories, and reading from your scriptures will enhance your experience here in the "Cradle of The Restoration."

SITES TO SEE

- **Hill Cumorah Visitors' Center** – This beautiful visitors' center, dedicated in 2002 by President Hinckley, is a great place to begin your visit in the Palmyra area. Allow at least one hour to tour the center, see the displays and hear the presentations. Be sure to pick up a handout on the significant events in the history of the Hill Cumorah and a very useful map of the restored historic sites both for this area and for Fayette. Of special interest are two videos you can view: "The Restoration" and "Joseph Smith – Prophet of the Restoration." Fourteen other videos, some in a variety of languages, are also available (most around 10-15 minutes in length). Children will enjoy the thirteen interactive exhibits. When standing in the Christus Room at night, notice that the reflection of Christ appears in each window panel. The visitors' center is open Monday thru Saturday 9 a.m.–8 p.m. in summer (but closes at 6 p.m. in winter and at 7 p.m. in fall), and Sunday 12:30 p.m.–8 p.m. in summer, (but closes at 6 p.m. in winter, and 7 p.m. in spring/fall). We suggest you check the web site to verify current/holiday hours. Notice that the visitors' center stays open one hour later than the other Church

Hill Cumorah Visitors' Center

sites. If time is short, consider visiting the other sites first and then finish here for a wonderful spiritual review. Restrooms are located here. The visitors' center is located next to the Hill Cumorah at 603 Route 21. For current information check their web site at www.hillcumorah.org or call 315-597-5851.

- **Hill Cumorah** –The angel Moroni first showed Joseph Smith the gold plates at this hillside on September 22, 1823. These ancient records contained a history of former inhabitants on the American continent. Forbidden to take the plates at that time, the young Prophet returned on the same date for the next four years to receive additional instruction. On September 22, 1827, Joseph returned with his new bride, Emma, who remained in the wagon while he climbed the hill to receive the plates. The center portion of the hill has been cleared of trees and is tiered to provide added staging for the Hill Cumorah Pageant which is performed annually in mid-July. A road on the left side of the visitors' center will take you to the top. Those wishing to walk can take a

Hill Cumorah

path located on either side of the hill. At the top you will find a grassy area with picnic tables. Overlooking the hill are benches providing a wonderful place to sit, read, and reflect. If you drive to the top, be sure to take a few minutes to walk down the path through the trees and part way down the hill. You can't help but feel the spiritual significance of this special site while standing here.

- **Angel Moroni Monument** – Moroni became the sole survivor of the great Nephite civilization, having seen his father and all his kinfolk slain in battle (Mormon 8:5). He buried the record of his people, written on gold plates, in the hillside of Cumorah around A. D. 421 and prophesied that these records would eventually be brought from the darkness into the light to shine forth (Mormon 8:16). It was this same Moroni who, as an angel, delivered the gold plates to the Prophet Joseph Smith in 1827. As you visit the monument, notice the embossed panels on all four sides, read the inscriptions and signs, and learn what the shaft, ornamentation, and lines of light on the monument represent. President Heber J. Grant dedicated the Angel Moroni Monument on July 21, 1935. As you sit at the monument, read some of Moroni's last written words to each of us. Feel the power of his testimony about the Book of Mormon and the sincerity of his plea for us to "come unto Christ" (Moroni 10:32).

- **Palmyra New York Temple** – In February of 1999, the announcement of the 100th temple was met with great joy in the "Cradle of The Restoration." The Palmyra Temple sits atop a hill overlooking the Smith family farm and Sacred Grove, bordering the towns of Palmyra and Manchester. At the groundbreaking ceremony, President Hinckley spoke of its special significance saying, "I regard this temple as perhaps the most significant, in one respect, in the entire Church. It was right here in the Sacred Grove where it all began" (Church News, May 29, 1999). President Hinckley dedicated the 10,700 square-foot temple on April 6, 2000. The temple's beautiful stained glass windows, depicting scenes from the Sacred Grove, and the white granite exterior add to its majestic beauty. During winter, the temple is closed on Sunday, Monday, and Wednesday. All sessions are by appointment only and there is no clothing rental available at this temple. For questions, to schedule a session, or to do baptisms, call 315-597-6001.

- **Welcome Center at The Joseph Smith Farm** – Your visit to the log home, frame home, Smith farm, and the Sacred Grove should begin here. Allow at least two hours to tour the two homes, visit the Sacred Grove and walk about the farm reading the many markers. Be sure to pick up a handout on the significant events that occurred at the Smith farm and a map showing the trails within the 10-acre Sacred Grove. (You can get lost, so use your map, watch your children, and notice the exit signs.) Restrooms are located here. All Church sites are open Monday thru Saturday 9 a.m.–7 p.m. in summer (but close at 5 p.m. in winter and 6 p.m. in spring/fall), and Sunday 12:30 p.m.–7 p.m. in summer, (but closes at 5 p.m. in winter, and 6 p.m. in spring/fall). Call for holiday/current hours. Remember that the Hill Cumorah visitors' center stays open later than the historical sites. Located at 843 Stafford Road. 315-597-1671.

- **Smith Family Log Home** – Joseph Sr., Lucy, and their nine children first lived in their 1 1/2-story log home from

Log Home

1818 until the fall of 1825 (their youngest child, Lucy, was born here). Some of the most significant events ever to occur took place in and around the small log home. Joseph went from this home into the woods to pray in the early spring of 1820 and received the First Vision. On the evening of September 21, 1823 and through the night into Sept. 22,

Upstairs Bedroom in Log Home

the angel Moroni appeared three times to Joseph Smith in an upstairs room. Later that day, Joseph went to the Hill Cumorah and first saw the gold plates. Less than two months later, the Prophet's beloved older brother Alvin died at this home on November 19, 1823. Hyrum and his wife Jerusha lived here from late 1826 through late 1830. Two of their daughters were born during their stay. After the financial loss of their frame home, the Joseph Sr. family moved back into the log home with Hyrum's family in the spring of 1829. The Smith log cabin was not only the hub of family life, it was also the center of Church activities going on in this area. Hyrum supervised the first printing of the Book of Mormon while living here. On a family visit from his home in Harmony, the Prophet received the revelations which are recorded in D&C 19, 22, and 23. The Smith family moved from this home in the fall of 1830. Joseph Sr. and Lucy lived for a brief time in Waterloo (near Fayette) before moving on to Ohio with the other Saints. Though the log home was eventually torn down or destroyed, it has been rebuilt on its original foundation and was dedicated by President Hinckley on March 27, 1998. As you walk through the rebuilt home, notice the small birthing room and imagine family life as it once was. Walk upstairs and read from Joseph's own words the account of his sacred experience (JS–H 1:29-54), and pause to reflect how much the spiritual events that occurred in and around this small log home have impacted each of us.

- **Sacred Grove** – On a beautiful spring day in 1820, fourteen-year-old Joseph went into the woods near the family's log home, seeking answers to his questions about religion. While Joseph was kneeling in prayer,

Sacred Grove

as directed in James 1:5, both God the Father and His Son, Jesus Christ, appeared and spoke to Joseph. Though Joseph would be persecuted for the rest of his life for his account of the First Vision, he would never deny what he knew to be true. Joseph said, "Why persecute me for telling the truth? ... For I had seen a vision; I knew it, and I knew that God knew it, and I could not deny it ..." (JS–H 1:25). Nine years later, after receiving the gold plates and completing their translation, Joseph was permitted to show these same plates to eight witnesses in the privacy of this sacred grove of trees (HC pp. 57-58). The benches located throughout the grove provide wonderful places to sit and read Joseph's account of the First Vision found in JS–H 1:5-20. As you walk through the Sacred Grove, take time to read the markers and feel the spiritual significance of this special area.

- **Smith Family Frame Home** – Alvin initially began construction on this New England style home in 1822. On his deathbed in November of 1823, he asked Hyrum

Frame Home

Kitchen

to see that the home was completed for their parents (HJS p. 116). Joseph Sr. and Lucy finally moved into their almost completed frame home towards the end of 1825. Unfortunately, they would have to leave this home in 1829 because of the dishonest actions of a neighbor, Russell Stoddard (for more details read HJS pp. 129-135). For the Smith family, the almost four-year stay in this home was full of both joyful events and difficult moments. In January of 1827, Joseph and his new bride, Emma, came here to live with the Smith family. On September 22nd of that same year, Joseph returned to the Hill Cumorah where he met with the angel Moroni and received the gold plates. When others sought to steal these plates, they were hidden for a time under the brick hearthstone in this home (HJS p. 149). After moving to Harmony, Joseph returned to his family home in July of 1828, concerned about the 116 translated pages that were entrusted to Martin Harris. As you look at the kitchen table, it isn't hard to visualize the Smith family gathered together while listening to Joseph tell of his incredible experiences or to imagine the Prophet as he sat at the kitchen table in almost inconsolable grief upon hearing Martin Harris report that the manuscript had been stolen (HJS pp. 164-166). Soon after, a new boarder at the Smith home, Oliver Cowdery, became an important help for Joseph as he continued the translation

Dry Sink

of the plates. In 2000, the original Smith frame home was restored as it was in the Smith family era. As you enter the home, notice to your left some of the original whitewashed wallboards, the replica of the wooden box used to hold the gold plates, the fireplace hearth under which the plates were once hidden, and a painted oilcloth rug. Lucy painted oilcloths that were used for tablecloths, blinds, and rugs. Joseph and Lucy's bedroom and sitting room, just to the right of the front door, has some of the original flooring. (Oliver and the Smith children slept upstairs.) In the kitchen, notice three items of luxury (but not the originals) that Lucy had in this home: the herb drying rack (notice that it is almost in the original location), a limestone dry sink, and the brick oven. Be sure to notice the small cutout portion of wallboard behind the kitchen table. You can still see the original dated newspaper used for insulation. Free guided tours of the frame home are given daily (schedule previously mentioned – Welcome Center at Sacred Grove). Restrooms are located behind the home. The frame home is located just a short walking distance south of the Smith log home.

- **Threshing Barn, Cooper Shop, Farm** – The 100-acre Smith farm is also referred to as the Manchester farm although the Smith log home actually lies just inside the Town of Palmyra. The reconstructed threshing barn and cooper shop (barrel-making) help you visualize the farm as it was during the Prophet's stay. The gold plates were once hidden in the loft of the cooper shop and though the building was ransacked by an angry mob, the hidden plates were not discovered (HJS p. 149). Take time to stroll around the farm and read the many informative markers. Imagine how hard the Smith family worked as they felled several thousand trees, nurtured their apple orchard, tapped over a thousand sugar maple trees and grew wheat, corn, and many other crops. Notice the rail fence around the perimeter of the farm. It was very common to stack stones below the fence rails as a barrier to livestock.

Cooper Shop, Frame Home, & Threshing Barn

- **William Stafford Home** – This is one of the few remaining homes from the Smith family era. The children of Joseph Sr. and Lucy attended school with the Stafford children. It is very likely that both the school and the road were named after the Staffords. The home is located at 405 Stafford Road (about 1.6 miles south from the Smith farm parking lot).

- **Porter Rockwell Home Site** – The Orin and Sarah Rockwell family lived less than two miles from the Joseph Sr. and Lucy Smith family. Their children attended school together and the two families became good friends. One of the Rockwell children, Orrin Porter Rockwell, forged a lifelong friendship with the 7 year older Joseph Jr. When Joseph and his parents would come to visit, Porter would beg his mother to let him stay up to hear the conversations. He

Porter Rockwell

even picked berries by moonlight and gathered wood to sell so that the proceeds could help print the Book of Mormon. Porter was an early convert and was baptized on April 6, 1830, the day the Church was officially organized (HC 1:79). Porter's colorful personality and his close friendship with the Prophet, fueled stories that were often part truth and part myth. Sometimes referred to as "the destroying angel" or "Joseph's bodyguard," Porter Rockwell was a pioneer, rancher, scout, deputy marshal, marksman, and a man of unwavering loyalty to friends. After the Prophet was martyred, Porter went west with the Saints and died of natural causes in Salt Lake City at the age of 65. The Rockwell home was probably located about 0.1 mile directly south of the Stafford home on Stafford Road.

- **Original Site of Stafford School** – The younger Smith children attended the Stafford School which was originally located at this site. In 1827, a young man named Oliver Cowdery was hired to teach at the school. He also boarded with the Smith family in their frame home (HJS p. 180). While residing with the Smith family, Oliver became well acquainted with the family and ultimately heard about Joseph's having received the gold plates. At this time, Joseph was living in Harmony with Emma. Wanting to meet the Prophet himself, Oliver went to Harmony where the two met for the first time on April 5, 1829 (HC 1:32). Two days after Oliver's arrival, Joseph recommenced translation of the Book of Mormon with Oliver acting as scribe. Oliver played an important part in early Church history, later becoming one of the Three Witnesses. The 1848 cobblestone building located at this site is not the original schoolhouse (see the following site for original building). It is privately owned and not available for tours. The Stafford School was located at 498 Stafford Road (about 2.1 miles south from the Smith farm parking lot).

Stafford School

- **Stafford District School House** – This is the original wood-framed Stafford Schoolhouse but it is not on the original site. (The original part of the school is the main section of the home.) The home is privately owned and not available for tours. It is located at 520 Stafford Road.

- **Corner of the Four Churches** – This interesting intersection of Church Street (Route 21) and Main Street (Route 31) was once listed in Ripley's "Believe It or Not." It is unique because a different church is located on each of the four corners. Though members of the Episcopalian, Baptist, Presbyterian, and Methodist faiths were all living here at the time the Prophet and his family also lived here, these four churches had not yet been built. The earliest church located at this intersection dates from 1832 (Presbyterian Church) and the Smith family had left the Palmyra area by the middle of 1831.

- **Dr. Alexander McIntyre Home** – One of the oldest homes in Palmyra is also the former home of Dr. Alexander McIntyre. He was the Smith family physician but was unfortunately out of town when Alvin first became ill. Upon his return two days later, Dr. McIntyre was one of the doctors who tried unsuccessfully to save Alvin's life and later helped perform the autopsy, discovering a gangrenous stomach blockage that caused his death (HJS p. 118). Later, as persecution against the Smith family increased, Lucy Smith recorded two separate occasions when Dr. McIntyre either chose not to participate or actually warned Joseph of the danger. As Joseph and Emma were planning to move to Harmony to work on the translation, a mob of 50 men made plans to stop the couple's departure and to seize the

"Gold Bible." The mob asked Dr. McIntyre to be their leader, but he refused (HJS p. 154). Several years later, when Joseph was about to leave for a meeting with E.B. Grandin, Dr. McIntyre came to warn the Prophet that a mob of 40 men was waiting to attack him. Dr. McIntyre had once again been asked to be their leader, and once

Dr. Alexander McIntyre Home

again, had refused. (HJS p. 203). The yellow home with white trim is located at 109 West Main Street (just to the left of the First Methodist Church on the northwest corner of the Main intersection). It is privately owned and not available for tours.

- **Book of Mormon Publishing Site** – In 1828, after the completion of the Erie Canal, a four-bay red brick building was constructed just east of the Main intersection. Several months later, E. B. Grandin rented the three-story westernmost bay for his printing and publishing business. Grandin's bookstore was located on the first floor; his book bindery and an office (rented by an attorney) were located on the second floor, while the print shop was located on the top floor. When Joseph first approached Grandin about printing the Book of Mormon, E. B. Grandin initially refused the job. He later consented to print 5,000 copies for $3,000 after some of his concerns were addressed and Martin Harris agreed to mortgage his farm to guarantee payment. The printing of the Book of Mormon began in August of 1829 and the first copies were finished on March 26, 1830. The 592-page book was sold at Grandin's bookstore for $1.25, a two-day wage in that day. On April 7, 1831, Martin Harris sold a large portion of his farm in order to make the agreed-upon payment. The first two bays of the original Grandin building have been purchased by the Church and have been restored. This site was dedicated by President Hinckley on March 26, 1998, the anniversary of the completion of the first printing of the Book of Mormon. Free tours are given daily (same hours as the other restored sites). Allow an hour stay to take the tour and learn about the detailed printing process, view an informative video, and see many historical objects including an original printer's proof sheet, two copies of the first-edition Book of Mormon, a representation of the Smith home in Harmony, and a replica of the single-pull Smith Patented Improved Press (original is in the Church Historical Museum in Salt Lake City). Notice the pulley system used to lower the print and the indentation left by the printer's feet in the original wood floor underneath the older

Smith Press

press. Children will also enjoy the interactive display on the main floor. Restrooms are located here. Be sure to pick up a handout on the significant events leading to the publication of the Book of Mormon. In addition, each family will receive a replica of an uncut sheet from the 1830 printed edition (not given out during pageant). Located at 219 East Main Street. 315-597-5982.

- **Pliny Sexton Home** – This home was built in 1827 and is one of the few homes remaining from the Joseph Smith era. Notice the historic marker in front of the building denoting that this home was used as part of the Underground Railroad system, which aided the escape of slaves in the Civil War period. Pliny Sexton's son, Pliny T., was born at this home in 1840. Pliny T. became a lawyer and ultimately owned many items of interest including the E. B. Grandin building, the original Smith press used to print the Book of Mormon, printer's proof sheets used in the first printing, and a portion of the land now referred to as the Hill Cumorah. The home is privately owned and not available for tours. It is located at 322 East Main Street.

Pliny Sexton Home

- **Palmyra Village Cemetery** – Persons of some note in Church history who are interred here include: E.B. Grandin (publisher of Book of Mormon), Harriet Rogers (Grandin's wife), other Grandin family members, John Gilbert and family (typesetter of Book of Mormon), Pliny T. Sexton (son of Pliny Sexton), Lucy Harris (wife of Martin Harris) and other members of the Harris family. Information can be obtained in the cemetery office on walking tours to see the above-mentioned graves and other sites of interest including the graves of Ambrose and Clarissa Hall, great-grandparents of Sir Winston Churchill. The cemetery is located on Vienna Street (which runs parallel to Main Street). To see E.B. Grandin's grave, go through the arched entrance and turn right on Linden Avenue. You will see a large obelisk monument with the name Frederick Smith on your left. It sits inside a small chained enclosure. Harriet's headstone is in the far left corner within this enclosure. Egbert is buried to her right.

- **Swift Cemetery** – This small cemetery was named after General Jonathan Swift (founder of Palmyra) who was killed during the war of 1812. His headstone is located in the middle of the grassy area. The modern granite headstone of Alvin Smith is on the far left side. Alvin was the oldest child of Joseph Sr. and Lucy and was idolized by his younger brother Joseph. In November 1823, Alvin became very ill.

Alvin Smith Headstone

Unable to find their regular doctor, the Smiths summoned another doctor who prescribed a dose of calomel (a laxative which was often given for a variety of ailments). Unfamiliar with the doctor, Alvin first refused to take the medicine but finally consented. Unfortunately, it lodged in his stomach and became gangrenous. After suffering for four days, Alvin passed away on November 19, 1823 at the age of 25. Knowing that he was dying, he counseled each of his siblings. To Joseph he urged "I want you to be a good boy and do everything that lies in your power to obtain the record. Be faithful in receiving instruction, and in keeping every commandment that is given you" (HJS p. 116). Although Alvin had not yet been baptized, Joseph later had a vision in the Kirtland Temple in which he saw his brother in the Celestial Kingdom (D&C 137). To view Alvin's headstone, climb the stairs located next to the blue and gold sign that says "First School House" and walk directly back along the left side of the cemetery.

(Notice the original marker is embedded in the back of the new headstone.) A Presbyterian church once stood in the area just to the south of Alvin's grave. Lucy Mack Smith and several of her children, including Hyrum, were members of this church before Joseph had the First Vision. Alvin's funeral took place at this church. The Swift Cemetery is located almost immediately north of the Main intersection, on the west side of Church Street, and across from St. Anne's Roman Catholic Church.

- **Original Section of Erie Canal** – While driving from Swift Cemetery to the Martin Harris Farm on Church Street, you will pass a section of the 1820 Erie Canal. The original canal was only 4 feet deep and 44 feet wide. Stop to see the canal or take a walk along the towpath where the mules walked as they pulled the boats. The original canal is located on the west side of the road about 0.2 miles north of the Main intersection. Just past the original canal, you will pass over a small bridge spanning the present-day Erie Canal. This canal was completed in 1918 and is 12 feet deep.

- **Martin Harris Farm** – Martin Harris once lived here in a 1 1/2-story white framed home. (His father, Nathan Harris, owned a large farm just a little further to the south.) New owners built the cobblestone home at this site after Martin's original home burned down in 1849. (You may notice several other cobblestone homes in the Palmyra/ Manchester area that were also built during this same period by the canal masons.) Martin first met the Smith family when he hired Joseph to work in the fields (for .50/ day), and Joseph Sr. and Hyrum to dig a well on his farm. After receiving a spiritual witness to the truthfulness of

Martin Harris Home Site

Joseph's work, Martin gave Joseph and Emma $50 to help them pay off their debts and move to Harmony to begin translation of the gold plates. Martin, more than twenty years older than Joseph, soon joined the couple in Harmony and served as the Prophet's scribe. In June of 1828, Martin was allowed to take the first 116 pages of translated manuscript back to his home in Palmyra with the promise that he would show the pages only to his wife and a few specifically mentioned individuals. However, Martin failed to keep his word as the manuscript was shown to additional people. Subsequently, the pages were stolen and never recovered. In her history, Lucy Mack Smith tells of the blessings Martin lost not only spiritually but temporally in consequence of his actions. "The same day on which the foregoing circumstance took place, a heavy fog swept over Mr. Harris's fields and blighted all his wheat, so that he lost about two-thirds of his crop, while the fields on the opposite side of the road remained untouched" (HJS p. 171). Though Martin did not act as scribe again, he did mortgage his farm to guarantee payment for the publication of the Book of Mormon and later sold 150 acres to make the $3,000 payment. Martin was privileged to be one of the Three Witnesses to the Book of Mormon. He was present when the Church was officially organized and was baptized the same day. After his wife died, Martin followed the Prophet to Kirtland, married a niece of Brigham Young, and marched with Zion's Camp. Martin ultimately left the Church in 1837, when many other prominent early members were also apostatizing, and did not go with his wife Caroline and their children to Utah. Remaining in Kirtland, he lovingly cared for the deserted Kirtland Temple, and was eventually rebaptized. At the age of 73, Martin crossed the plains to rejoin his family in Utah. He died on July 10, 1875, having never denied his written testimony as one of the Three Witnesses. The Martin Harris farm is located 1.5 miles north of the Main intersection at 2095 Maple Avenue (Church Street turns into Maple). The home is owned by the Church but is not available for tours.

- **Lucy Harris Home** – Martin married Lucy, his first cousin, in March of 1808. Though Martin believed Joseph to be a Prophet of God, Lucy did not. She was critical of both the time and money spent by her husband to help Joseph with the translation. It is very likely that she was involved with the theft of the 116 manuscript pages entrusted to her husband. Martin's involvement in the Church, culminated by the loss of a large portion of their farm to pay off the $3,000 printing payment, led to a final separation between Lucy and Martin. She and the children moved to this two-story farm home, situated on about 80 acres, which was deeded over to her by Martin in

1825. She died at the age of 44 in the summer of 1836 and is buried in Palmyra Village Cemetery. To see the home, continue past the Martin Harris farm 0.5 miles and turn left at Macedon Center Road. Continue 0.4 miles west and you will see the white two-story framed home on your right at 2827 Macedon Center Road. It is privately owned and not available for tours.

THINGS TO DO

- **Hill Cumorah Pageant** – Don't miss the experience of seeing this high technology, multi-tiered production with a cast of over 700 costumed performers. The pageant is held on the hillside just to the right of the visitors' center. Scheduled for July 9, 10, 13-17 in 2010 (Check www. hillcumorah.org for 2011). The pageant starts at 9:15 p.m. (begins filling up by 7 p.m.) and is free to the public. Tickets not required.

- **Canaltown Days** – A local celebration held in Palmyra on the third weekend in September. Festivities include a parade, antique show, many outdoor activities, and lots of great food. The Wayne County Fair is held at the fairgrounds in August as is Pirate Weekend. Check www. palmyrany.com for exact dates and details.

- **Aqueduct Park & Lock #29** – This is a great park for picnics, biking, enjoying the beautiful scenery, and to see a lock on the Erie Canal. Though the original canal had over 80 locks, the newer canal has fewer than half that number (33 state locks). If you're lucky, you may see the locktender at work helping a boat through the lock. We found the tenders very knowledgeable and

Original Aqueduct

willing to answer all of our questions. Children will enjoy the free Erie Canal activity book available at the locktender's small office next to the canal. Also notice the remains of one of the original aqueducts built in 1856 over Ganargua Creek. When the original Erie Canal had to cross over a river, an aqueduct was built to route the river beneath the canal. To locate the park, drive west on Main Street about 0.7 miles from the Main intersection. The entrance to the park will be on your right, next to the "Town of Macedon" sign. After entering the park you will see a recently restored 1858 crossover bridge to your right; the aqueduct and children's playground is to your left. To see the Erie Canal and Lock #29, walk across the one-lane bridge located north of the parking lot.

Lock #29

- **Alling Coverlet Museum** – Did you know that Martin Harris was an accomplished weaver, had 13 looms, and won several awards for his work? In fact most of the weavers during this time period were men. This museum features the largest collection of hand-woven coverlets in the country (none made by Martin). Also displayed are about 200 quilts and miniature rugs, and an on-site gift store. Open daily 1 p.m.–4 p.m., from June 1 thru September, or by appointment. Located at 122 William Street (near Grandin Bldg.) 315-597-6981.

- **William Phelps General Store Museum** – Step back in time as you enter this general store once owned by William Phelps (no relation to W.W. Phelps). The 1890s grocery store remains almost as he left it – including the original eggs in their carton. The tour of the upstairs family living quarters on the second floor is interesting. Open Tuesday thru Saturday, 1 p.m.–4 p.m. from June thru mid September, or by appointment. Located at 140 Market Street. 315-597-6981.

- **Print Shop Museum** – In 1860, John Jones began a printing business which continued for the next 63 years. See the original Palmyra-made Platen Printing Presses, learn about the printing process, and enjoy hands-on activities. Open Tuesday thru Saturday, 11 a.m.– 4 p.m. from June 1 thru mid September, or by appointment. Located at 138 Market Street. 315-597-6981.

- **Palmyra Historical Museum** – Once a hotel, this museum features many items from Palmyra's past including village records, furniture, military items, children's toys, etc. Notice the special Smith family exhibit called "Life in Palmyra 1820-1840." Open

Tuesday thru Saturday, 11 a.m.– 4 p.m. on weekends from June thru mid September, or by appointment. Located at 132 Market Street. 315-597-6981.

- **Admission for the previously listed museums** – Ailing Coverlet, William Phelps Store, Print Shop, and the Historical Museum is $2/adult (per museum), $1.50/ senior (per museum), and $1/child (per museum). If you are planning to see several of the museums, we suggest you purchase the Trail Ticket (admission to all museums) for $5/adults, $3/seniors and $2/children. Also consider the Family Trail Ticket for $10 (2 adults/3 children). *Free gift (large map of 1870 Palmyra) to those who purchase the $5 or $10 trail tickets. **D**

- **Village of Fairport** – A quaint village built around the Erie Canal. Notice the one-of-a-kind 1912 liftbridge spanning the canal on Main Street. Not only is the south end of the bridge higher than the north end, no two angles in the bridge are the same. Park near the bridge and enjoy a leisurely stroll along the canal.

Village of Fairport

- **Colonial Belle** – Cruise the Erie Canal on the largest boat offering sightseeing and dining cruises on the canal. Choose lunch, dinner or sightseeing only. Daily departures

Tuesday–Saturday, mid-May through October. The 2-hour cruise is $15, 3-hour cruise is $18, lunch cruise $26, and dinner cruise is $33. Visit www.colonialbelle.com or call 585-223-9470. **D**

- **Canandaigua Lady** – To cruise Canandaigua Lake on an authentic replica of a 19th century paddlewheel steamboat, call 585-396-7350.

- **Roseland Waterpark** – On hot days, this waterpark can be very inviting. Enjoy a wave pool, slides, tube rides, and the raft rider. Open June 15 thru Labor Day. Admission: adults/$21, children/$16 (ages 4-10), seniors over 60/$5. Located at 250 Eastern Blvd., Canandaigua. 585-396-2000.

- **Sonnenberg Mansion and Gardens** – This 50-acre estate includes a 40-room 1887 Victorian mansion and nine formal gardens featuring water fountains, statues, reflecting pond, on-site café, and gift shops. Open daily from mid-May thru October. Admission: adults/$10 and students/$5. Located at 151 Charlotte Street, Canandaigua. 585-394-4922.

- **Sodus Bay Lighthouse** – Stop at Sodus Bay Lighthouse and then enjoy a picnic at the nearby beach/park along Lake Ontario. Though the original lighthouse was built in 1825, the lighthouse standing today was erected in 1870 and was in operation until 1901. Free tours are given at the lighthouse museum. Open Tuesday – Sunday, 10 a.m.–5 p.m. from May thru October. Located at 7606 North Ontario Street. 315-483-4936.

- **Sportworks Family Fun Park** – Featuring two miniature golf courses, big swing golf range, batting cages, ice cream shop, and café. Open mid March thru mid October. Located at 180 Route 31, Macedon. 315-986-4245.

- **County Line Raceway** – Go-kart raceway located across the road from Sportsworks. 315-986-5876.

- Things to do in nearby **Rochester** include: Seabreeze Amusement Park, Six Flags Darien Lake, George Eastman House, National Women's Hall of Fame, Rochester Museum and Science Center, Susan B. Anthony House, Seneca Park Zoo, and the Strong Museum (nation's leading hands-on history center).

PHOTO SPOTS

- **Hill Cumorah Visitors' Center** – As you stand in the parking lot facing the visitors' center, look to your right and you will see a "large" Book of Mormon. It makes a fun backdrop for a picture.

- **Angel Moroni Monument** – For a group photo with angel Moroni, have your family stand in front of the monument (we stood on the bench). To take the picture, walk down the small flight of stairs to the platform just below and take the shot looking up at the monument. You should be able to get a head shot of your group with angel Moroni in the upper background.

- **Hill Cumorah** – There are many special photo opportunities at this site. They include a panorama shot of the hill taken from the bottom right corner next to the parking lot, one at the top looking down (especially beautiful at sunset), and many as you walk along the wooded path.

- **Palmyra Temple (distant shot)** – You will get a great picture of the Palmyra Temple while walking from the Smith log home towards the Smith frame home. About half-way between the homes, stop and take a picture of your family as they stand against the rail fence with the temple nestled in the trees as your background.

- **Palmyra Temple** – We found that the best photo angle for the temple is up on the hillside next to the parking lot (left side). The stained glass windows, lit by the sun, make another great picture.

- **Aqueduct Park** – There are many interesting and picturesque sites here including the old aqueduct, the Erie Canal, and numerous family photo spots within the park (see things to do – Aqueduct Park and Lock #29).

- **Fairport Harbor, Canandaigua Lake, and Sodus Point** are all picturesque spots. Be sure to have your camera handy.

- For professional pictures taken of you and your family at the Sacred Grove, Hill Cumorah, etc., contact Jim at Miranda Photography. 315-359-9001.

LDS CHURCH SERVICES

A beautiful LDS Stake Center was completed in 2002. It is located across the street from the Palmyra Temple at 2801 Temple Road. Sacrament Meeting begins at 9 a.m. for the Palmyra Ward. Additional wards are located in Canandaigua, Fayette, Fairport, and Lyons. Check www.lds.org for current information.

ATM

An ATM is located one block east of the Main intersection at the HSBC Bank on East Main Street. The Ontario National Bank is located further east on Main Street near the post office. Additional ATMs can be found in several convenience stores and the IGA Grocery Store.

SHOPPING

For those who enjoy shopping for antiques, gifts, homemade candy, souvenirs, crafts, books, or artwork – you are in luck! You will find all this and more as you stroll Main Street in downtown Palmyra. Two large shopping malls are also located in this region.

- **Latter-day Harvest Bookstore** – This full service LDS bookstore is your one-stop store for LDS books and more. Other items of interest include framed art, statues, souvenirs, and many other gift items. In addition to everyday discount prices, show this guidebook and receive a free gift (one gift per book). Open Monday thru Saturday from 10 a.m. to 6 p.m. Located next to the E. B. Grandin building at 213 East Main Street. 866-553-3600. **D**

- **Candy Corner Fudge Square** – For those with a sweet tooth – enter at your own risk! Enjoy fresh made candy, fudge, and cookies. Notice the unique LDS-themed chocolate bars. In addition to tasty treats, the store has gift items and more. Open Monday thru Saturday, 10 a.m. – 5 p.m. Located at 205 East Main. 315-597-6636. **D**

- **Brick House Antique Center** – Enjoy browsing for quality antiques in this two-story 1860's brick store. Shipping is available and credit cards are accepted. Open year round; Monday thru Thursday 10 a.m. – 4 p.m., Friday & Saturday 10 a.m. – 6 p.m. and Sunday noon – 4 p.m. Located at 247 E. Main. www.brickhouseantiques.com or 315-597-3883. **D**

- Enjoy the **farmer's market** held every Saturday (during the summer) from 8 a.m. until noon at the village park located on east main between the Main intersection and the E. B. Grandin building.

- **Waterloo Premium Outlet Center** – Over 100 outlets stores including Polo, Ralph Lauren, Liz Claiborne, Eddie Bauer and more. Also includes on-site food court, and ATM machine. Located in Waterloo (take exit 41 on I-90 to Route 318 West or exit 42 to Route 318 East). 315-539-1100.

- **Eastview Mall** – Premier shopping with Kaufmann's, Lord & Taylor, Sears, Target, Home Depot, and over 170 other shops. Also includes on-site food court and 12-screen cinema. Located west of Palmyra at 7979 Pittsford-Victor Road, Victor. 585-223-4420.

- **Wal-Mart** – The closest Walmart is located in Lyons on Route 31 (about 10 minutes east of Palmyra).

RESTAURANTS

You will find numerous dining choices in Palmyra as well as other selections in nearby towns including Newark, Canandaigua, Macedon, Fairport, and Victor. Check www. hillcumorah.org or www.palmyrany.com for additional restaurant and lodging choices.

PALMYRA

- **Mark's Pizzeria** – Popular pizzeria where the dough is made fresh daily and your food is made to order. Large menu selection including pizza, salads, calzones, wings, subs, pasta dishes, and hamburgers. We thought the pizza was tasty and affordably priced. Delivery to Palmyra and Macedon available. Conveniently located at 240 East Main Street. 315-597-2727. **D**

- **Yellow Mills Diner** – Enjoy a country breakfast, homemade soups and daily chef specialties. Featuring delicious chicken & biscuits, prime rib, and jumbo fish fry. We enjoyed our roast turkey dinner w/dressing for $8. Serving breakfast, lunch, and dinner, Monday thru Saturday 6 a.m.-9 p.m. and Sunday 7 a.m.-2 p.m. Located at 2534 Route 31. 315-597-4613. **D**

- **Chill & Grill** – Recommended by locals and visitors alike, this fast food stand has the ultimate huge ice cream cone (try the kiddie size w/3 scoops) and the interesting Garbage Plate (ask what's in it). Open April thru September. Located at 616 East Main Street. 315-597-8946.

- **Nima's Italian Restaurant** – Tasty pizza, sandwiches, and more. My calzone was delicious and large enough to feed two people (checks or cash only). Located at 165 E. Main Street. 315-597-5399.

- **Muddy Waters** – Open at 6:30 a.m. on Tuesday thru Saturday; serving breakfast and lunch. 100 Division Street. 315-502-4197.

- **Brad & Dads** – Featuring homemade ice cream. Located at 623 E. Main. 315-597-0116

- **Subway** – Located at 510 E. Main.

- **Happiness Garden** – Enjoy this eat in or take-out Chinese restaurant. Located at 212 E. Main Street. 315-597-8868.

- **Akropolis** – 513 Canal Street, 315-597-5634.

- **Athenia Restaurant** – 606 East Main Street. 315-597-4287.

- **IGA (Grocery Store)** – Has a bakery, deli sandwiches, salads, and prepared hot dishes with microwave available to heat. Located on East Main Street at the intersection of Route 31 and Route 21 North.

NEWARK

To go to Newark from Palmyra, drive east on Main Street and continue on Route 31 for about 9 miles. Located here is lock 28-B on the Erie Canal. This area also holds some early Church historical significance.

In 1830, twenty-three-year-old Parley P. Pratt and his wife, Thankful, were traveling from the Kirtland, Ohio area to eastern New York, by way of the Erie Canal. As they neared Newark, Parley felt impressed that he should disembark. Though not sure why, Parley got off at Newark while Thankful continued on. Parley soon heard about a new book of scripture called the Book of Mormon. After acquiring a book, Parley read it all day and night, wanting little sleep or food. Hungry for more knowledge about this book, he went to the Smith log home and met Hyrum Smith. Parley and Thankful were soon baptized in Fayette. Parley's nineteen-year-old brother, Orson Pratt, also joined the Church.

Newark also has a variety of dining choices. Some of them include:

- **Tom Wahl's** – Locally known for its homemade root beer and large hamburgers. Located at 585 West Union. 315-331-9112.

- **Mark's Pizzeria** – Pizza chain restaurant previously mentioned in Palmyra. Located at 535 West Union Street. 315-331-4974.

- **The Corner** – Popular local fast food diner located at the corner of Route 31 and Route 88.

- **Cross Park Family Restaurant** – Family-friendly with a variety of menu options. Located at 1121 E. Union Street (Route 31). 315-331-9120.

- **Wegmans** – A premier grocery store that is well known for its fresh produce, delicious gourmet foods, and inviting atmosphere. The deli offers a wide variety of homemade items including soups, salads, pasta, sandwiches, or pizza. Stop in for the ultimate supermarket experience. Located at Miller & Finch Streets. 315-331-4440.

- **Additional choices include:** McDonald's, Wendy's, Subway, Pizza Hut, and Burger King. Most are located along West Union Street.

CANANDAIGUA

Canandaigua is located about 15 miles south of Palmyra on Route 21. The village is nestled next to Canandaigua Lake and offers not only picture perfect scenery but also holds some Church historical significance.

William W. Phelps was first introduced to the Church while living in Canandaigua. He worked as an editor on a local newspaper and purchased a Book of Mormon just a few days before the Church was officially organized. After reading the book, he went to see the Prophet in Fayette. William and his family later moved to Kirtland where he joined the Church. We still sing many of the hymns he wrote including "The Spirit of God," written for the dedication of the Kirtland Temple and "Praise to the Man," written in honor of the Prophet Joseph Smith.

The Prophet's father, Joseph Smith Sr., was imprisoned in Canandaigua for 30 days in October 1830. A Quaker gentleman came to Joseph Sr. demanding payment on a $14 note (bill). Lucy offered all the money she had ($6), with a promise to soon pay the rest, or her gold beads that were worth more than was owed. But the man said that only if Joseph Sr. were to burn all copies of the Book of Mormon in his possession, would the debt be forgiven. Joseph Sr. refused to comply and was consequently taken to Canandaigua where he was confined. Lucy did relate one positive result of this experience. Joseph Sr. preached during his confinement and after his release, he baptized two individuals who had been converted (HJS p.179-186).

Canandaigua has a variety of dining choices. Some of them include:

- **Lehigh Valley Family Restaurant** – Wide variety of menu options. Open daily from 5 a.m.–10 p.m. Located between Palmyra and Canandaigua, at the intersection of Routes 96 & 21. 585-289-3684.

- **Wegmans** – Premier grocery market and café as mentioned in Newark. This is a great stop to buy fresh produce, pizza by the slice, or deli sandwiches for a picnic at the lake. Located at 345 East Boulevard. 585-394-4820.

- **Fast food choices include:** McDonald's (Parkway Plaza), Taco Bell, Mark's Pizzeria, Ponderosa Steakhouse, Arby's (Eastern Blvd.) TCBY (Eastern Blvd.), and KFC (South Main).

MACEDON

Located west of Palmyra on Main Street about four miles from the Main intersection.

- **Flaherty's** – Missionary recommended for lobster bisque, steak, and prime rib. Located at 113 Pittsford Palmyra Road. 585-223-1221.

- **Miceli's Restaurant** – Serving dinner only and specializing in steak, prime rib, and seafood. Located at 1011 Route 31. 315-986-2954.

- **Macedon Hills Family Restaurant** – Serving breakfast, lunch, and dinner with large menu variety. Located at 1090 Pittsford-Palmyra Road. 315-986-5836.

- McDonald's, Subway Sandwiches, and Burger King are also located on Route 31.

FAIRPORT

To reach Fairport from Palmyra, drive west on Route 31 for about 11.7 miles and turn right on Route 250 North.

- **Arrivederci's Pizza & Subs** – Restaurant owner Sebastian makes a tasty eat-in or take-out pizza. Located at 55 South Main Street (ATM located next door). 585-425-2898.

- **Lickety Splits** – Ice cream and "udder" great stuff located at 6 North Main. 585-377-6250.

- **Other dining choices include:** Pizza Hut, McDonald's, Wendy's, Ruby Tuesday, Applebee's, Bill Gray's, Boston Market, Papa John's Pizza, and Zoe's.

VICTOR

Located about 15 miles southwest of Palmyra and very close to the villages of Fishers and Mendon (see Mendon). Take exit #45 on I-90. Located here are Eastview Mall and many dining choices including:

- **Pizzeria Uno** – We first discovered and enjoyed this pizza-chain restaurant in Boston. 585-223-6100.

- **Other choices include:** Houlihan's (585-223-4680), Friendly's, Chili's, Denny's, Burger King, Ruby Tuesday's (585-223-2260), and Applebee's (585-425-4700).

LODGING

While there are only a few lodging choices in Palmyra, a wide range of hotels and B&B's can be found in surrounding towns. Rates posted are seasonal and subject to change. Please verify pricing before making your reservation.

PALMYRA

- **Palmyra Inn** - Built in 2005, the inn features 60 rooms with kitchenettes; includes some handicap equipped rooms and suites. Basic room rates start at $99 w/ continental breakfast included. Enjoy high-speed Internet access in each room, guest laundry, jacuzzi/exercise room, elevator, on site convenience store, computer station, and two large meeting rooms. Located just minutes from the

Sacred Grove at 955 Canandaigua Road. 800-426-9900 or www.palmyrainn.com. **D**

- **Liberty House B&B** – Victorian home built in the 1870s, conveniently located in the heart of Palmyra Village. Offers main floor guest room with private bath and two second-floor guestrooms with shared bath. Rooms range from $89 to $99 with Irene's gourmet breakfast included. Newly released missionaries that are with their parents stay free! Located at 131 West Main Street. For more information, visit www.libertyhousebb.com or call 315-597-0011. **D**

NEWARK

- **Quality Inn Finger Lakes Region** – Full service hotel situated near the historic Erie Canal. Includes 107 rooms/ suites with rates starting at $79. Featuring indoor heated pool with garden atrium, fitness center, and on site restaurant. Located six miles from Hill Cumorah, at 125 North Main Street. Call 315-331-9500 or visit www. qualityinnnewark.com. **D**

CANANDAIGUA

- **Super 8** – Offering 50 rooms including king suites with whirlpool baths. Room rates starting at $75 with light continental breakfast included. Located 15 miles from Palmyra, near all types of dining, and within walking distance to scenic Canandaigua Lake, at 350 Eastern Blvd. 585-396-7224. **D**

- **Econo Lodge Canandaigua** – Located just one block from Canandaigua Lake, at 170 Eastern Boulevard (Routes 5 and 20). 585-394-9000.

- **Bed & Breakfast at Oliver Phelps** – Federal style historical home featuring five well appointed bedrooms with private baths, great food, and funny but flexible innkeepers that will cater to your needs. Rates start at $120 and include full breakfast. Located at 252 N. Main Street. Contact Jack and Donna at www.oliverphelps.com or call 585-396-1650. **D**

- **Canandaigua Inn on the Lake** – Lakeside inn featuring 134 rooms, indoor/outdoor pools, and on-site restaurant. Located at 770 South Main Street. 800-228-2801.

FAIRPORT/ PITTSFORD

- **The Lodge at Woodcliff** – Relax and enjoy the breathtaking vista at this full service resort property set on top of Rochester's Bristol Hills. Featuring indoor/outdoor heated pool, fitness center, 9-hole golf course, on site restaurant, and 244 rooms/suites starting at $169. Located at 199 Woodcliff Drive, Fairport. For more information, visit www.woodclifflodge.com or call 800-365-3065. **D**

- **Brookwood Inn** – Located at 800 Pittsford-Victor Road, Pittsford. 800-396-1194 or 585-248-9000

VICTOR

- **Hampton Inn & Suites** – Newer property situated in a park-like setting with 123 guestrooms including 55 suites. Featuring fitness center, indoor pool with whirlpool, convenience shop, and free local calls. Room rates starting at $129 with deluxe continental breakfast buffet included. Located just 15 miles from Palmyra at 7637 State Route 96. Visit www.rochesterhamptoninn.com or call 585-924-4400. **D**

- **Springdale Farm Bed & Breakfast** - A quaint B & B in a rambling 19th century farmhouse. Featuring four remodeled guest rooms with private bath, air conditioning, and cable TV. Room rates start at $129/night with full breakfast included. Located about 12 miles from Palmyra at 242 Country Road 9, Victor. www.springdalefarmbb.com or 585-924-5952. **D**

ROCHESTER

- Rochester is located just 24 miles northwest of Palmyra. You will also find a wide variety of lodging choices there.

CAMPING

- **KOA Campground of Canandaigua** – Scenic location, sites with full hook-ups, shady tenting area, swimming pool, playground, laundry facilities, cabin rentals, convenience store and more. Located at 5374 Farmington Townline Road, Canandaigua. 800-KOA-0533 or 585-398-3582.

- **Wayne County Fairgrounds** – Tent and RV sites are available during the months of July and August. Located at 250 West Jackson Street, Palmyra.

Notes

Notes

Notes

Notes

Notes

Notes

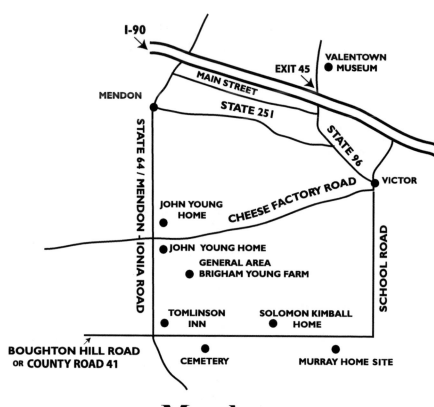

Mendon

Chapter Fifteen
Mendon

Brigham Young and Heber C. Kimball are familiar names to Latter-day Saints, but few are aware that many of the sites and some of the significant events in their early church years are located in and around Mendon, New York. Here a lasting friendship was forged between the two future leaders of the Church. Located about 20 miles southwest of Palmyra, Mendon is a brief but worthwhile stop.

In 1827, John Young (Brigham Young's father) moved from Tyrone, New York and settled in this area. Other members of the Young family also relocated to Mendon including Brigham, Joseph, Phineas, and their families. At the nearby Tomlinson Inn, Samuel Smith first introduced the gospel to the Young family. Many of these were later baptized including Brigham and his wife Miriam. Only a few months after baptism, Miriam died at the age of 27 and was buried in Mendon.

Heber C. Kimball moved into this area in the early 1820s. He worked as an apprentice in his brother's pottery shop and later purchased the business. Heber and his wife Vilate were also introduced to the gospel and baptized here. They would soon become a strong support for a grieving Brigham and his two young daughters after Miriam's death.

PLANNING YOUR TIME

Allow one hour or more to walk around the small cemetery and visit the suggested sites. Most are in close proximity to each other. If you follow the suggested route, you will make a rectangular shaped loop of about 30 miles.

GETTING THERE

Driving on I-90, take exit 45 heading south. On your way to Mendon via State 96, turn west onto County Road 42 (Main Street) and you will go through the village of Fishers. Several sites mentioned are located here on Main Street. To see the other sites in Mendon, continue south on State 96 until it intersects with State 251. Turn right on State 251, heading west. Mendon is located at the intersection of State 251 and State 64. Turn left on State 64, heading south. You will see the John Young home at the intersection of State 64 and Cheese Factory Road. Continue south on State 64 and turn left onto Boughton Hill Road (also marked as County Road 41). Many of the sites are found while driving east on Boughton. To return to I-90, turn left at the intersection of Boughton Hill Road and School Road, heading north. At the intersection of School Road and State 96 (you are now in the Village of Victor), turn left on State 96 and head west. Continue on State 96 heading northwest until it intersects with I-90.

SITES TO SEE

Fishers is located about 2 miles northeast of Mendon. It was named after the Fisher family, early settlers who built several local mills. Brigham Young worked in this area as a carpenter. His brother, Phineas also lived here for a short time. Credit for the location of these sites goes to Sheldon Fisher, a local historian who spent many years researching and preserving the history of this area. Sheldon passed away in January of 2003 at the age of 95. He was a delightful person and is greatly missed.

Sheldon Fisher

- **Woolston-Fearnside Home** – Tradition says that this home was built by Brigham Young in 1829. It is located at 7864 North Main in Fishers. The home is privately owned and not available for tours.

- **Charles Fisher Homestead** – It is believed that Brigham cut and glazed the windows on the east side of this 1811 two-story home. Charles Fisher first settled this area and later bought craft work from Brigham Young. He attended the Mendon Baptist Church, as probably did Brigham Young and Heber C. Kimball. By the early 1830s, many from the Baptist church became converts to the restored gospel and were baptized in Brigham Young's millpond. It is also believed that early missionaries held meetings in this home. The Fisher home is located at 7868 North Main Street. It is privately owned and not available for tours.

- **Phineas Young Home** – Tradition says that Phineas Young (Brigham's brother) lived for a short time in the home located at 8026 North Main Street. Phineas was born in 1799 and moved to this area to be near his family in 1829. Samuel Smith, Joseph Smith's younger brother, first introduced Phineas to the gospel. He was baptized the same day as his father (John Young) on April 5, 1832. His brother, Joseph, was baptized the following day. The home is privately owned and not available for tours.

As you continue further south from Fishers, you enter the township of Mendon. Drive by the suggested sites and walk around the cemetery. Be sure to take a few minutes to walk across the street from the cemetery for a great panoramic view. It will help you visualize the proximity of the existing homes and sites.

- **John Young Home** (front portion of home) – The original home of John Young (Brigham Young's father) has been separated into two homes. The front portion of the home is located at 981 Cheese Factory Road, while the back portion of his home is across the street. An old barn was once located near this home. The barn was dismantled and

John Young Home (Front)

the wood was used to build the threshing barn located at the Joseph Smith family farm in Manchester. The home is owned by the LDS Church but is not available for tours.

- **John Young Home** (rear portion of home) – John Young served in the Revolutionary War under George Washington. In 1783, he married Abigail Howe and they were the parents of eleven children. They named their ninth child Brigham after one of his great-grandparents. Abigail died when Brigham was just fourteen years old. John Young arrived in Mendon with his second wife, Hanna Brown, in 1827 and eventually purchased over 50 acres of land. Many of his children also relocated here including Brigham and his wife Miriam, who built their home on part of John's land. It is believed that Brigham built this home for his father and lived here until his own home was completed. John was baptized on April 5, 1832, moved to Kirtland, Ohio in June of 1833, and died in Quincy, Illinois on October 12, 1839. His home originally stood here at 984 Cheese Factory Road. Today the front portion is not the original (look across the street and imagine the two halves together), but the back of the home is. The Church also owns this property but the home is not available for tours.

John Young Home

- **Brigham Young Home Site and Mill** – The site of Brigham's home was by a small stream located southeast from his father's home. Brigham, his wife Miriam, and their young daughter Elizabeth moved to Mendon in the spring of 1829. He built a two-story house with the mill in the lower section and their home on the top. Brigham was a carpenter by trade and the small stream with a dam located next to the home was sufficient to turn the water wheel that operated his lathe. Soon after their arrival, a daughter Vilate was born on June 1, 1830. Around this same time, Brigham Young first saw a copy of the Book of Mormon that had been given to his brother Phineas. It would take Brigham almost two years of study before he was ready to be baptized in the stream by his home on April 15, 1832. His wife Miriam was baptized about three weeks later. Soon thereafter she became very ill with tuberculosis and Brigham took over the responsibilities in the home. He would feed the children and carry Miriam to a rocking chair each morning before he left. Upon returning, he cleaned, fixed dinner, and took care of Miriam and the two young daughters. She died at the age of 27 on September 8, 1832. Shortly after Miriam's death, Brigham went to visit the Prophet in Kirtland and later went to Canada to preach the gospel. During his absence, Brigham's two daughters, Elizabeth (age 7) and Vilate (age 2) went to live with Miriam's niece and her husband, Vilate and Heber C. Kimball. In September of 1833, Brigham and his daughters moved to Kirtland, Ohio.

- **Tomlinson Inn** – Constructed in 1810, the Tomlinson Inn was once an important stagecoach stop on a three-day route that went from Canandaigua to Buffalo. In April 1830, while

stopping here to have dinner, Phineas Young met Samuel
Smith (Joseph Smith's brother). Samuel presented Phineas
with a Book of Mormon explaining, "There is a book, sir,
I wish you to read." Samuel also promised that if Phineas
read it with a prayerful heart, he would receive a witness
of its truthfulness. Not only did he read it, but so did many
members of his extended family. Phineas, his father John,
brothers Joseph and Brigham, his sister Fanny, and the six
other brothers and sisters and spouses all read the Book
of Mormon and eventually joined the Church. Though all
the siblings later experienced hardships and persecution,
none ever apostatized. The innkeeper, Nathan Tomlinson,
also joined the Church. His inn became a meeting place
for missionaries, members, and investigators. After the
Mendon Branch was organized in 1832, the inn was used
as their gathering spot and place of worship. The Mendon
Branch initially numbered over thirty members including
many of the Young siblings' families, Heber C. Kimball
and his family, the Tomlinson family, the Barlow family,

Tomlinson Inn

and others. The Tomlinson Inn is located at 473 Mendon-Ionia Road (Route 64). The elongated portion on the east side of the home is the original portion of the inn. Members of the Church own this home and permission is given to walk the grounds.

• **Heber C. Kimball Home and Pottery Works Site** – Heber's home was located just to the east of the Tomlinson Inn. He moved into this area in the early 1820s. Though originally trained as a blacksmith, he also worked as an apprentice at his brother's pottery shop and eventually purchased the business. Heber married Vilate Murray in 1822, first met Brigham Young in 1829, and later went with Brigham in November 1831 to Phineas Young's home to hear missionaries teach about the restored gospel. Just six months later, in April 1832, Heber was baptized in the small millpond by Brigham's home. Vilate was baptized two weeks later. She also took care of Miriam during the last few weeks of her life; Miriam passed away in their home. Heber and Vilate continued to take care of Brigham's children after Miriam's death. The Kimball's moved to Kirtland in the fall of 1833. Like the clay he once molded, Heber's life would be shaped by future experiences. He was like clay in the hands of the potter as he participated in Zion's Camp, left his family to serve a mission in England on two occasions, defended and remained true to Joseph when other prominent members apostatized, and served as a counselor to Brigham Young. His life was one of dedication to the gospel. His grandson, Spencer W. Kimball, would serve as the 12th President of the Church. The owners of the Tomlinson Inn also own Heber's home site. Permission is given to walk the grounds.

- **John and Rhoda Young Greene Home Site** – Though the exact location of this home is also unknown, we do know that it was very close to Heber's home because of an experience that was later recorded. Rhoda was a sister of Brigham Young and the following passages have been taken from *Life of Heber C. Kimball* by Orson F. Whitney. Heber recounts, "I had retired to bed, when John P. Greene, who was living within a hundred steps of my house, came and waked me up, calling upon me to come out and behold the scenery in the heavens. I woke up and called my wife and Sister Fanny Young (sister to Brigham Young), who was living with us, and we went out-of-doors" (p.15). Heber further records that they witnessed an army, marching in platoons from the east to the west. "No man could judge of my feelings when I beheld that army of men, as plainly as ever I saw armies of men in the flesh.... After I became acquainted with Mormonism, I learned that this took place the same evening that Joseph Smith received the records of the Book of Mormon from the angel Moroni, who had held those records in his possession" (pp. 16-17).

- **Tomlinson Corners Cemetery** – In the southwest corner of this very small cemetery is the gravesite of Miriam Young. Also buried here are Heber's parents, Solomon F. Kimball and Anna Spaulding Kimball. As you face the cemetery, the graves are located in the first row on the far right side. The Church has placed

Solomon Kimball Headstone

a newer headstone marking Solomon's grave with the original stone imbedded in the front. Other members of Heber's family buried here include: Judith M. & Roswell Heber Kimball (children of Heber

Miriam Young Headstone

and Vilate; exact burial location unknown), Charles & Judith Kimball (brother and sister-in-law, buried next to Solomon Kimball), and Susannah Murray (Vilate's mother; exact burial location unknown). Walk across the street for a great view of the surrounding area. See if you can locate the Tomlinson Inn, John Young's home, and the general area of Brigham's home site. The cemetery is located on the south side of Boughton Hill Road about 0.4 miles east from the State 64/Boughton intersection.

- **Solomon Kimball Home** – Solomon F. Kimball and his wife, Anna Spaulding, were the parents of seven children. He was the father of Heber C. Kimball and the great-grandfather of Spencer W. Kimball. Solomon died of tuberculosis on July 8, 1825. His wife Anna had preceded him in death, also from tuberculosis. The Solomon Kimball home is located about .4 miles further east of the cemetery at 933 Boughton Hill Road. It is privately owned and not available for tours.

Solomon Kimball Home

- **Roswell and Susannah Murray Home Site** – Continue about 2.2 miles further east from the Kimball home and you will pass the area of Vilate Murray Kimball's childhood home. Heber first stopped here in the summer of 1822. While riding his horse, he became thirsty and stopped to ask a man working in his yard for a drink. This man, Roswell Murray, called to his daughter to bring a glass for the stranger. Heber was so taken with her that he lingered as long as possible by drinking the water as slowly as he could. It wasn't long before he frequently took rides down this same road and always became "thirsty" and stopped. Heber and Vilate, or "my-Laty" as he often called her, were married on November 7, 1822. Vilate was 17 years old. After Susannah's death, Roswell Murray married Fanny Young (Brigham Young's sister) in 1832. The Murray home was once located at what is now 406 Boughton Hill Road. The home now standing at this site is not the original home.

If time allows, an interesting stop is a small museum located in Valentown just northeast of Fishers and on the north side of I-90. Stop here before starting the loop or finish here after returning from Mendon for a great finale of this area.

- **Valentown Museum** – There are several items to note inside this small museum. Notice a chair made by Brigham Young, bricks and other artifacts excavated from his home, some of his tools, and a drawing showing what his home and mill looked like. In this same room are several things that have been excavated from other sites in the area as well as historical documents. Credit for the artifacts and for the museum goes to Sheldon Fisher. He is also responsible for several items currently displayed in the Church History Museum in Salt Lake including Brigham's wooden lathe and pottery made by Heber C. Kimball. Open Sunday Noon – 4, June thru October. Admission: $4/adult, $3/children. The Valentown Museum is located about .4 miles north of I-90 exit 45.

Valentown Museum

Coming from Mendon on State 96, continue north past the I-90 onramp. The museum/store will be on your right. www.valentown.org or 585-924-4170.

Notes

_____

_____

_____

_____

_____

_____

_____

_____

_____

_____

_____

_____

_____

_____

_____

_____

_____

_____

_____

_____

Notes

Chapter Sixteen
Niagara Falls

One of the most beautiful natural wonders in North America is located in the western portion of New York. Though it was once thought of as a "honeymoon" destination, over 12 million tourists now visit each year to view the thundering Horseshoe and American Falls. In 1953, Marilyn Monroe starred in a movie featuring this location entitled *Niagara*. Christopher Reeve also "flew" through the area while filming *Superman II*. While some have successfully defied nature by going over the falls in a variety of contraptions, most are content to experience the force of over 750,000 gallons of water per second by observation tower or by boat.

Though Niagara Falls could not be considered an L.D.S. Church site, early Church members including Joseph Smith, John Taylor, and Parley P. Pratt did pass through this area. On October 10, 1833, Frederick G. Williams sent a letter from Kirtland to the Saints in Missouri mentioning that Joseph Smith and Sidney Rigdon had gone "down the lake to Niagara, from thence they expect to go into Upper Canada, as far as Long Point, and preach in all the most noted places on their way" (HC 1:418). Parley P. Pratt, called on a mission to Upper Canada, saw the falls for the first time in 1836. Inspired by their beauty, Brother Pratt wrote a poem that included the lines, "O, Niagara! Generations may pass in long succession; ages may roll away and others still succeed; empires may rise and flourish, and pass away and be forgotten; but still thy deafening, thy solemn and awful voice is heard in one eternal roar" (*Autobiography of Parley P. Pratt* p. 131).

GETTING THERE

Niagara, situated about 20 miles northwest of Buffalo between Lake Erie and Lake Ontario, actually spans the border between the United States and Canada. Traveling from Kirtland (about 200 miles away), take I-90 east towards Buffalo, New York (about 166 miles). Take exit 53 to I-90 N. (for about 22 miles) and watch for the signs.

Coming from Palmyra (about 100 miles away), take I-90 west towards Buffalo (80 miles). Merge onto I-290 west, via exit 50 towards Niagara Falls, and follow the signs.

From Buffalo, take I-290 to I-90 going across Grand Island to Route 62. Once you get close, just follow the signs.

PLANNING YOUR TIME

If you have never visited Niagara Falls and are traveling between Kirtland and Palmyra, or vice versa, consider making a detour up to the falls. Depending on your time – spend a few hours here before leaving for your next destination, make this a day-trip excursion from Palmyra, or spend a day and stay overnight.

If time is short, stay on the American side. See the falls from the observation tower, walk down the stairs beside the American Falls, take a ride on the Maid of the Mist, or visit Goat Island. If time allows, cross over to the Canadian side for a more complete view of the American and Horseshoe Falls. Reading the activities/sites section will help you to plan your time. Remember to watch your children closely when near the water. Though very beautiful, the water can be very inviting but dangerous for small children. Weather can also be unpredictable; remember to wear good walking shoes and bring an umbrella or rain poncho. We have found that depending on the current exchange rate, it can be more economical to spend the night on the Canadian side. (Remember to get your room tax rebate at the duty free shop.) In the evening, don't miss seeing the falls colorfully lit from dusk until midnight each night (until 10 in winter). You can also enjoy the fireworks display over the falls each Friday and Sunday evening at 10 p.m. during the summer months.

VERY IMPORTANT: Effective summer of 2009, passports are required for those traveling to and from Canada. For questions, call 716-282-3141.

NIAGARA FALLS

The Niagara Falls are the second largest falls in the world, with Victoria Falls in Africa being the largest. One-fifth of all the fresh water in the world is found in this Upper Great Lakes region. The four upper lakes (Michigan, Huron, Superior and Erie) all flow and eventually empty into the Niagara River and ultimately cascade over the falls. From the falls, the water continues its course about 15 miles further before reaching the last of the Great Lakes – Ontario.

The word "Niagara" is taken from the Iroquois language meaning "the strait". Though we usually refer to only the American and Horseshoe Falls, there is actually a small third fall located next to the American Falls – Bridal Veil Falls. The two falls located on the U.S. side rise to a height of 176 feet and produce a flow of water of about 150,000 gallons/second. The larger Horseshoe Falls on the Canadian side produces over 600,000 gallons of water per second. Power plants located upstream channel some of the water for hydroelectric use.

American Falls, Bridal Veil Falls and Horseshoe Falls

The first person attempting a ride over Horseshoe Falls was a 63 year-old schoolteacher named Annie Taylor. In October 1901, she went over the falls in a wooden barrel and survived. Of the sixteen known attempts made to go over the falls in barrels, 10 individuals are thought to have survived.

ACTIVITIES/SITES TO SEE

Contact the Niagara Falls Visitors Bureau at 800-421-5223 or the State Parks at 716-278-1770. Call 800-338-7890 to request a free visitors guide or request online at www.niagara-usa.com. Visit www.niagarafallslive.com for more detailed information, to verify current admission fees, and for live pictures of the falls. Contact the Canadian Visitors Tourism Center at 800-563-2557 to request a free visitors guide or contact the Canadian Parks at 877-642-7275 or 905-356-1303 for information about guided walking tours. Visit www.discoverniagara.com for more detailed information about sites, lodging, restaurants, and shopping on the Canadian side. Some discount passes for Niagara Falls attractions are available on this site.

There is often a long wait during July and August at some of the more popular tourist sites and attractions. I suggest you plan to visit them either early morning or late afternoon to avoid the wait. A shuttle bus system stops/starts at numerous locations along the American side of the falls. Cost is $2/day for adults and $1/children. A similar shuttle service is available on the Canadian side.

- **Niagara Falls State Park and Visitors' Center** – This park was established in 1885 and is the oldest state park in the United States. Walk along the upper Niagara River and see the rapids just before they continue over the American Falls. In the visitors' center, park rangers can answer your questions, provide maps, and help you to plan your time. (If you are spending the entire day here – ask about the Passport to the Falls.) Take a few minutes to enjoy the hands-on displays. A 40-minute IMAX film can be seen in the Festival Theater. The cost is $11/adults and $7.50/children. Café, restrooms and gift store are located here. The State Park is open from 7 a.m.–10:15 p.m. year round. Admission to the park is free but there is a parking fee of $10/day. 716-278-1796.

- **Observation Tower at Prospect Point** – Located inside Niagara Falls State Park. This is the best spot on the American side to view the falls, gorge, and Rainbow Bridge. Ride the elevator down to the base and take the stairs to the "crows nest" next to the cascading falls. A $1 fee is charged for entrance to the tower/elevators. Boat rides on the Maid Of The Mist begin here at the base of the falls. (Your admission ticket for the boat ride includes the $1 fee.)

- **Maid Of The Mist** – Enjoy a 30-minute cruise along the base of the American Falls and return via the bend at Horseshoe Falls. Plan to be heavily "misted" by the 30-minute experience – everyone receives a rain poncho. Cruises can be taken from both the American and Canadian sides. Open daily from May thru October (check exact date) 9:15 a.m.–8 p.m. (off season 10 a.m.-5 p.m.). Admission: adults/$13.50, children 6-12/$7.75. Tickets are purchased at the observation tower. 716-284-8897.

Maid of the Mist in front of American Falls

- **Cave Of The Winds** – Guided walking trip along special walkways for those who want to get the total "misting" experience at the base of the American Falls. Open May thru October 9 a.m.–7:30 p.m. Admission: adults/ $11, children (6 –12)/$8. (Everyone receives a free pair of sandles.) 716-278-1730.

- **Goat Island** – Perfect area for a picnic or a picturesque stroll in the park. Visit Terrapin Point or visit the Three Sisters Island for a great view of the Niagara River and Horseshoe Falls from the American side. Open year round.

- **Niagara Gorge Discovery Center** – See a short video presentation explaining the geological making of the gorge and falls and learn more about the local and natural history through the interactive learning centers and displays. Open April thru October 9 a.m.–5 p.m. (stays open till 7 p.m. in the summer). Admission: adult/$3 and children/$2 Located .5 mile north of the falls on Robert Moses Parkway. 716-278-1780.

- **Aquarium of Niagara** – Enjoy sharks, moray eels, sea lions, piranha, penguins and other aquatic animals. Open year round 9 a.m.-5 p.m. Admission: adults/$9, children/$6. Located at 701 Whirlpool Street. 800-500-4609 or 716-285-3575.

- **Rainbow Bridge** – Most will cross over from the American side to the Canadian side on this bridge via I-190. You may cross by auto, foot, or bicycle. Admission: cars/$3.50 (round trip) and pedestrians/$.50. During peak season, there may be a wait to cross; consider taking the Whirlpool Bridge or Lewiston Bridge.

Rainbow Bridge

The following activities and sites are located on the Canadian side. For your convenience, admission prices are listed below in American dollars and not to be confused with the Canadian dollar admission listed at the sites. (It is hard to be exact as the exchange rate changes.) Almost every site or restaurant listed will take American currency or credit cards.

- **Queen Victoria Park** – Stroll through this beautiful park situated along the gorge for a great view of Rainbow Bridge, Horseshoe Falls and the gorge. The park is open year round and admission is free.

- **Maid Of The Mist** – Same boat ride as previously mentioned except you board this boat in Queen Victoria Park. Information center also located here. There are often longer lines on this side. Most tour groups arrive early – for a shorter wait, consider going in the late afternoon. Open mid April thru October, daily 9 a.m.-7:45 p.m. (off season 9:45 a.m.-4:45 p.m.) 905-358-5781.

- **Journey Behind The Falls** – For those that want a behind the falls "misting" experience. Located at the Table Rock Complex next to Horseshoe Falls. Open daily, May thru October 9 a.m.–5:30 p.m. (open until 10:30 p.m. in summer). Admission: adults/$12, children/$7.25 (online discounts availavle). 905-354-1551.

Successfully made it over the falls

- **IMAX Theatre Niagara Falls** – Experience the history, myths, rapids, heroic acts and death-defying stunts via the largest film format. See a collection of barrels that have made it over the falls. National Geographic Store and Pizza Hut Express also located inside. Open year round. Admission: adults/$11.50, children/$8.50 (on-line discount available). Located at 6170 Fallsview Blvd. 905-358-3611.

- **Skylon Tower** – Enjoy a bird's eye view of the entire area from either the indoor or outdoor observation deck situated 775 feet above the falls. Open year round, summer 8 a.m.–midnight and winter 9 a.m.–10 p.m. Admission: adults/$11, children/$7. Located at 5200 Robinson Street. 888-366-9297 or 905-356-2651.

- **Marineland Theme Park** – Enjoy marine shows, an aquarium, hands-on activities and park rides. Open May thru October. Admission: adults $36, children $30. Located 1 mile south of Horseshoe Falls at 7657 Portage Road. 905-356-9565.

- **Dufferin Islands** – For a picnic spot, picture perfect bird watching, and numerous hiking trails, visit this nature preserve located less than 1 mile south of Horseshoe Falls. Open daily from dawn to dusk. Admission is free.

- **Niagara Spanish Aero Car** – See the spectacular whirlpools, rapids, and Niagara gorge suspended high above in a cable car. Open year round. Located about 3 miles north of Horseshoe Falls. 905-354-5711.

- **Niagara Parks Butterfly Conservatory** – Enjoy the world's largest glass enclosed butterfly conservatory at the Niagara Parks Botanical Gardens. Café, gift shop and restrooms also located here. Open year round.

Admission: adults/$12, children/$7. Located 5 miles north of Horseshoe Falls. 905-358-0025.

- **Niagara Parks Botanical Gardens** – Featuring 100 acres of manicured formal and informal gardens and arboretum (famous for its large collection of roses). Open year round and admission is free. Located 5 miles north of Horseshoe Falls.

PHOTO SPOTS

There are many photo spots at Niagara Falls. My biggest challenge is trying to limit the number of pictures taken! We purchase a disposable waterproof camera to take pictures while out on the boat and at other "misty" sites.

- You can take a great family picture, with the American Falls in the background, while standing at the "crows nest" at the base of the Prospect Point observation deck.

- The best pictures of the American Falls are taken on the Canadian side. We found a great photo spot for a family picture just to the right after exiting from our boat ride.

- You can't beat the view or the panoramic pictures taken from the observation deck at the top of the Skylon Tower. I especially enjoyed the photos taken late at night showing the colorfully lit falls.

LDS CHURCH SERVICES

The Buffalo Ward meets at 780 Michigan and Goodell Road in Buffalo, New York. Sacrament meeting begins at 9:30 a.m.

On the Canadian side, the St. David's Ward meets at 785 Warner Road, Niagara-on-the-lake. Sacrament Meeting begins at 9:30 a.m. Check at www.lds.org for updated information.

ATM

An ATM is located on the American side at the HSBC Bank on Niagara Street. ATMs are located on the Canadian side at the Table Rock Complex, Maid of the Mist, and in several of the larger hotels.

For lodging, dining, and other purchases made on the Canadian side, try to use a credit or debit card for ease and to get a fair exchange rate. The most convenient location for currency exchange is at the Royal Bank or at the Niagara Duty Free Shop. Both are located on the Canadian side, just after crossing Rainbow Bridge. There are several banks along both Lundy's Lane and Queen Street. Be aware that some stores may offer to exchange currency but their rates will probably not be as good as bank rates.

SHOPPING

There are several shopping malls on the American side including:

- **Prime Outlets at Niagara Falls** – Enjoy a huge selection of outlet shopping including Old Navy, Guess, Tommy Hilfiger, and Polo. On-site restaurants include Applebee's, and Red Lobster. Located at 1900 Military Road (take exit 22 on I-190). 800-414-0475 or 716-297-0933.

- **Rainbow Center Factory Outlet Mall** – Located at 302 North Rainbow Boulevard.

There are many gift stores and several malls on the Canadian side. Remember to save your Canadian receipts. You may be entitled to a tax refund and you will be required to declare your purchases before entering the U.S. (Visit the Duty free shop by Rainbow Bridge for any questions or help.) For U.S. custom questions call 716-881-4447.

- **Niagara Duty Free Shop (and G.S.T. refund center)** – Enjoy perfume, chocolate and other duty free shopping here. Bring your original receipts showing the G.S.T. (Goods and Service Tax) here to receive your refund. Your G.S.T. total must be $14 (Canadian dollars) or more on lodging, dining, clothing, souvenirs, etc. to qualify for refund. Call for the latest information at 877-642-4337 or 905-374-3700. In order to receive the refund, this must be your last stop before departing Canada. The Duty Free Shop is located just before crossing Rainbow Bridge at 5726 Falls Avenue.

- **Table Rock Complex** – An information center, first aid station, stroller and wheelchair rentals, restrooms, restaurants, photo supplies, and numerous souvenir stores can be found in this large complex next to Horseshoe Falls.

- **Victoria Park Gift Shop** – Featuring one-of-a-kind gift and souvenir items. Located on River Road in Victoria Park. 905-371-0254.

- **National Geographic Store** – One of only three such stores in the world, this store is located inside the Imax Theater building. 905-358-3611.

- **Canada One Factory Outlets** – Many outlet stores. To exchange money, visit Thomas Cook located inside the mall. 7500 Lundy's Lane. 905-356-8989.

- You will find **souvenir stores** at most of the local attractions including Maid of the Mist, Butterfly Conservatory, Niagara Spanish Aero Car, and Floral Clock.

RESTAURANTS

- **Top of the Falls Restaurant** – Open during the summer and located on Goat Island. 716-278-0340.

- **Hard Rock Café** – Located close to Rainbow Bridge at 333 Prospect Street. 716-282-0007.

- You will also find a variety of **restaurants** located in "Little Italy" around Pine Avenue (62 A).

On the Canadian side:

- **Table Rock Restaurant** – Overlooks Horseshoe Falls in the Table Rock Complex. Enjoy lunch, dinner (early dinner menu is discounted) and children's menu. Also located in the Table Rock Complex: ice cream, pizza, and other fast food choices (most are cash only).

- **The Secret Garden Restaurant & Gift Shop** – Enjoy either inside or outside dining for breakfast, lunch, or dinner. Menu options include sandwiches, hamburgers, pasta, salads, children's menu and a vegetarian menu. Located across the street from the Casino Niagara at 5827 River Road. 905-358-4588.

- **Skylon Tower Restaurants** – A revolving restaurant is located on top with entrees starting at $37. The Summit Suite buffet-style restaurant on the level below offers a buffet lunch (adults $25) and a dinner buffet. 877-474-6317 or 905-356-2651.

- You will find a variety of restaurants and fast food choices in and around the central sites including Hard Rock Café, Planet Hollywood, and Rainforest Café.

- You can also find a large selection of local dining and fast food choices along Lundy's Lane including McDonald's, Red Lobster, Dairy Queen, and Denny's. On Clifton Hill you will find a Ruby Tuesday's, Boston Pizza, and Wendy's. An Applebee's is located at 6546 Buchanan Avenue.

LODGING

There are many lodging choices on the American side. Check the previously mentioned web sites for a more detailed selection. Some of the AAA rated lodgings include:

- **Comfort Inn/The Pointe** – Includes 118 rooms. Located at 1 Prospect Pointe.

- **Hampton Inn Niagara Falls** – Featuring indoor pool and fitness room. Located minutes from the falls at 501 Rainbow Boulevard. 800-426-7866.

- **Four Points Sheridan Inn** – Featuring 189 guest rooms. Located at 114 Buffalo Avenue. 716-285-2521.

- **Red Coach Inn B&B** – Chosen as a top 10 getaway site by Fortune Magazine, this English Tudor retreat offers

15 rooms overlooking the Niagara rapids. Continental breakfast included. Located at Two Buffalo Avenue. 716-282-1459.

There are also many choices near the Buffalo airport including: Buffalo Hampton Inn, Four Points Buffalo Airport, Radisson Hotel and Suites, and Marriott Hotel. You will find many lodging options on the Canadian side. Some include:

- **Sheraton On The Falls** – Featuring 670 luxury rooms with on-site fitness center and four restaurants. Located directly across from the falls at 5875 Falls Avenue. 888-229-9961 or 905-374-4445.

- **Brock Plaza** – Includes 233 guest rooms, indoor pool and on-site restaurant. Located next to the Sheraton at 5685 Fallsview Blvd. 800-263-7135.

- **Hampton Inn At The Falls** –127 guest rooms, indoor pool and continental breakfast. Located one block from the falls at 5591 Victoria Ave. 800-688-3535.

- **Holiday Inn By The Falls** – Located at 5339 Murray Street. 905-356-1333.

- **Marriott Courtyard** – Located at 5950 Victor Avenue. 905-358-3083.

- **Marriott Fallsview** – Located at 6740 Fallsview Blvd. 905-357-7300. (we stayed here)

- **Chestnut Inn** – Built in the late 1800s, this colonial home overlooks the gorge and has been featured in several commercial photo shoots. Deluxe continental breakfast included. Located at 4983 River Road. 905-374-7623.

CAMPING

- **Niagara County Camping Resort (American side)** – This camping and RV park has 240 sites with extras including: showers, camp store, beach, 2 private lakes, 3 playgrounds, and more. Located at 7365 Wheeler Road. 716-434-3991.

- **Niagara Falls KOA (American side)** – Enjoy two heated pools, playground, laundry facilities, and grocery store. Located at 2570 Grand Island Boulevard. (Take exit 19 on I-190 north and follow the KOA signs.) 800-562-0787 or 716-773-7583.

- **Niagara Falls KOA (Canadian side)** – Features include two outdoor and one indoor pool, playground, pavilion, grocery store, laundromat, and game room. Located 3 miles from the falls at 8625 Lundy's Lane. 800-562-6478 or 905-354-6472.

- **King Waldorf's (Canadian side)** – Includes laundry facilities, showers, heated pool, and playground. R.V. sites with full hook-ups and tent sites. Located close to the falls and Marineland at 9015 Stanley Avenue. (Campers receive discount admission to Marineland.) 905-295-8191.

Notes

Notes

Notes

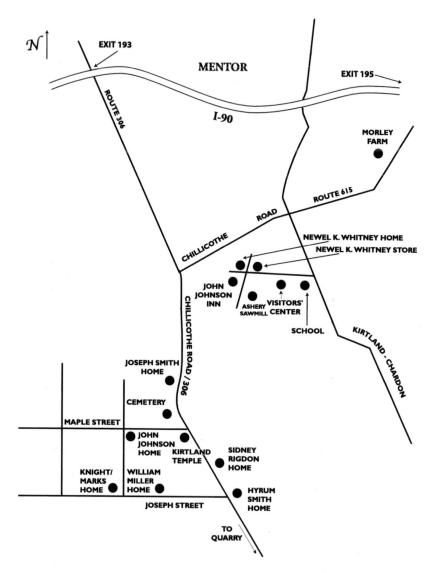

HISTORIC KIRTLAND SITES

Ohio   ***Chapter Seventeen***
Kirtland

Kirtland, often called the "City of Faith and Beauty," lies about 22 miles east of Cleveland in the northeast corner of Ohio. Located less than 7 miles from Lake Erie in the Lake County district, the city of Kirtland offers a wealth of Church historical sites, nature reserves, and beachfront recreation.

In 1811, a former Revolutionary War soldier named Christopher Crary along with his wife Estella and nine children became Kirtland's first permanent settlers. Among other early settlers to the area was a man named Isaac Morley. By the early 1820s, a township had been created and buildings were erected including a sawmill, gristmill, and schoolhouse. Another early settler, Newel K. Whitney, opened Kirtland's first general store in 1823. Several years later, Newel also became the local postmaster. By 1827, Kirtland had its first hotel – the Peter French Inn. About this time, a young man from New York named Parley P. Pratt settled in Amherst, just 45 miles west of Kirtland. He became good friends with and accepted the teachings of a Reformed Baptist minister named Sidney Rigdon. Impressed that he should share his newfound beliefs, Parley sold his farm in Amherst and returned to New York with his wife only to hear about and discover a new book of scripture called the Book of Mormon. While reading it, wanting little food or sleep, Parley felt an assurance of its truthfulness. Hungry for more knowledge, he went to Palmyra where he met Joseph Smith's brother, Hyrum, and was soon baptized.

In October 1830, Parley P. Pratt was one of four missionaries called in New York to go west and teach the gospel to the Lamanites (D&C 32:1-3). They taught as they traveled to the western Missouri region. Parley stopped in the Kirtland area to share the gospel with his friend, Sidney Rigdon. Sidney was skeptical, but allowed Parley and the other missionaries to preach to his congregation. In a few weeks, the four missionaries succeeded in converting and baptizing 127 individuals before continuing on their journey. Some of these new converts included Sidney Rigdon, Isaac Morley, Lyman Wight, Newel K. Whitney, Frederick G. Williams, John Murdock, and Philo Dibble. Edward Partridge was also taught by these early missionaries and was later baptized after visiting the Prophet in Palmyra.

While the Church was growing in the Kirtland area, the Saints in Palmyra were facing persecution. In December 1830, and again in January 1831, Joseph was directed by the Lord: "... go to the Ohio…" (D&C 37:3, D&C 38:32). In February 1831, the Prophet and his family arrived in Kirtland, thus establishing it as the headquarters of the Church. In the next few months, many of the Saints in New York sold their farms, often at a loss, and joined the Prophet in Kirtland. During the next seven years, from 1831 to 1838, Church membership in the area grew to about 2,000. But of even greater importance were the many significant spiritual events that occurred in and around Kirtland during this important period in Church history.

PLANNING YOUR TIME

As your read this chapter, you will probably be surprised at the many important sites in and around Kirtland. To appreciate the significance of this area, we suggest you plan for a two-day visit. (Trying to see it all in one day would be a very rushed experience.) Begin at the LDS visitors' center and take the walking tour that includes the schoolhouse, sawmill, ashery, Whitney Store, Whitney home, and Johnson Inn. Other "must see" sites include the Morley farm, the Kirtland Temple, and the John Johnson farm in Hiram. "Nice to see" sites include the quarry, Fairport Harbor, North Kirtland Cemetery, and still-existing homes of early Church members. If time allows, drive by some of these homes, and visit several of the other local attractions included in this chapter.

GETTING THERE

If you are coming from the East (Palmyra) on I-90, take exit #195 (Route 615 exit). Turn left and travel on Route 615 for about .4 miles. When you come to the T stop, turn right. You will pass the Morley Farm on your right. Turn left at the signal (Kirtland/Chardin Road). The LDS visitors' center will be on your right.

If you are coming from the West (Cleveland) on I-90, take exit #193 (Mentor and Kirtland/Route 306 exit). Continue south and follow the Historic Kirtland signs. The Kirtland Temple is about one mile south on Route 306 (also known as Chillicothe Road) while the LDS visitors' center is also nearby on Kirtland-Chardon Road, near the intersection of Routes 306 and 615.

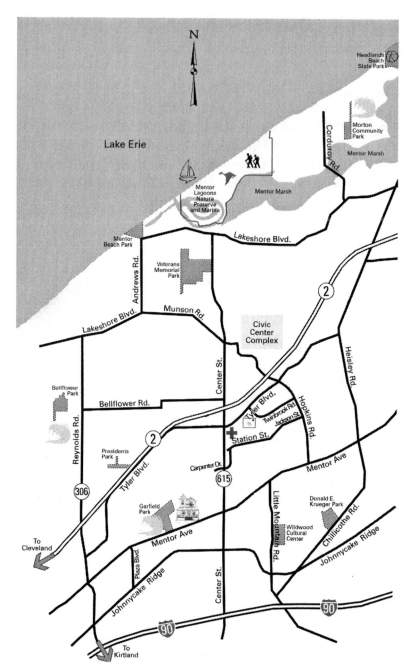

MENTOR

Courtesy City of Mentor

SIGNIFICANT EVENTS

It is difficult to describe even briefly all of the significant events that occurred during the Kirtland Period from 1831 to 1838. Among these are the following: almost one-half of the revelations recorded in the Doctrine and Covenants were received here, the first edition of the Doctrine and Covenants was published, the organization of the Church headed by the First Presidency and Quorum of the Twelve was established, the first stake was organized, the School of the Prophets was started, Joseph Smith's inspired revision of the Bible was completed, the first temple in this dispensation was built, and many marvelous spiritual manifestations were experienced.

Visiting the sites mentioned in this chapter, reading the brief synopses, taking the tours of the homes, and reading further from some of the suggested sources will help you to more fully understand the significance of the Kirtland period in the history of the Church.

KIRTLAND TEMPLE

The Kirtland Temple stands majestically atop the hill as a reminder of the sacrifices made by the early Saints while constructing this important edifice. When Joseph received the commandment to build the temple, the Church and its few hundred members were struggling financially. But despite their individual hardships, the Saints were united in building the House of the Lord. Men began plowing and preparing the land at the temple site soon after the revelation was received.

The dimensions for the temple were also received by revelation, as was its purpose. The lower part was to be used "for your sacrament offering, and for your preaching, and your fasting, and your praying, and the offering up of your most holy desires unto me," while the higher part was to be used "for the school of mine apostles" (D&C 95:14-17).

The first cornerstone of the temple was laid on July 23, 1833. Work progressed quickly as stone was chiseled from the nearby quarry and lumber was cut at the sawmill. Women made clothing for the temple workers and even donated their glassware, which was crushed to add sparkle to the exterior plaster. Though construction was greatly slowed by the formation of Zion's Camp and the trek to Missouri, the temple was completed in less than three years.

Close to 1,000 people attended the dedication of the Kirtland Temple on March 27, 1836. The dedication service included the sacrament, testimonies, and the unanimous sustaining of Joseph Smith and the Twelve Apostles. Many songs were sung including "Adam-ondi-Ahman," and a special song written for this sacred occasion, "The Spirit of God." In the dedicatory prayer, the Prophet spoke of the work that was done through great tribulation in order to "build a house to thy name, that the Son of Man might have a place to manifest himself to his people" (D&C 109:5). Several speakers at the dedication testified that angels were in attendance, while others who were present recorded that heavenly manifestations were both felt and seen. A repeat dedication took place on March 31. (Read the Prophet's account of the Kirtland Temple dedication in HC 2:410-428 and the Kirtland Temple dedicatory prayer in D&C 109.)

Just one week later, on April 3, 1836 (Easter Sunday), the Savior appeared to Joseph Smith and Oliver Cowdery in the temple. He told them: "For behold, I have accepted this house, and my name shall be here; and I will manifest myself to my people in mercy in this house" (D&C 110:7). The Prophet recorded that on that special Sabbath day, in addition to the Savior, three other Personages appeared who restored important keys of the Priesthood: Moses, Elias, and Elijah. About three months later, Joseph received another revelation in the temple as recorded in D&C 112. (Prior to the dedication, Joseph had also received a revelation in the temple now recorded in D&C 137.) Once the center of activity for Church members, the temple was abandoned in 1838 as the Saints again faced persecution and continued west. Tours of the Kirtland Temple, owned by the Community of Christ (formerly RLDS), begin in the Community of Christ visitors' center located next to the temple. The temple's interior has been restored and is inspiring. The exterior of the Kirtland Temple is also in excellent condition and the grounds are beautiful.

SITES TO SEE

• **LDS Visitors' Center** – Constructed in the style of a gristmill, the visitors' center is a wonderful place to begin your tour. Notice the photo gallery with pictures of early Kirtland, see the large mural of the Kirtland Temple being built, and view some of the more recently restored sites (sawmill, ashery, inn, etc.) through a glassed-in observation room. This area is excellent for those limited in their mobility or on stormy days. There are two videos available to view: "Joseph Smith's Kirtland" and "Joseph Smith – Prophet of the Restoration." While you are here, be sure to pick up several informative handouts and brochures. Open Monday thru Saturday 9 a.m.–7 p.m. and Sunday 11:30 a.m.–7 p.m. (closes at 5 p.m. in winter). Free guided walking tours of the sites in this immediate area are provided daily. Restrooms are located here. Allow 90 minutes or more to stop at the visitors' center and to take the walking tour of the nearby sites, now referred to as Historic Kirtland Village. (If time is short, consider taking a tour of the Kirtland Temple first.

Historic Kirtland Visitors' Center

It closes at 5 p.m.) The visitors' center is located at 7800 Kirtland-Chardon Road, near the intersection of Routes 306 and 615. www.visithistorickirtland.com or 440-256-9805

• **Schoolhouse** – The rebuilt schoolhouse is located on the same site where the original 1819 schoolhouse once stood. Learn more about the education process in the early 1800s and compare it to our education system today. Not only a school, the building was also used for city council meetings, as a poll during elections, and as a church. Early Saints met here on Sundays for sacrament meetings. Joseph was probably referring to this building when he recorded, "In the evening I preached in the school house, to a crowded congregation" (HC 2:301). You will find the building in front of the entrance to the LDS visitors' center.

• **Sawmill** – Don't forget to stop at the rebuilt sawmill located behind the visitors' center. Joel Hills Johnson built the original water-powered sawmill in 1834. Lumber cut at the mill was used in the construction of homes,

Ashery and Sawmill

businesses, and the Kirtland Temple. The sawmill also provided much-needed employment for new converts moving into the area.

• **Ashery** – Rebuilt on the original site, the ashery was important for both practical and financial reasons. Newel K. Whitney originally owned the ashery and the Saints would sometimes bring their ashes to his store in trade for goods. These ashes were mixed with water and processed into very marketable and desirable products called pearl ash and potash. While you are here: discover the purpose of the ashery, find out why it was so important to the Saints, discover why hardwood trees made the best ashes, learn about the process, and be surprised at what products were made from the end result. The ashery is located next to the sawmill and is the first of its kind to be restored in North America.

- **Tannery** – The home located just to the right of the Newel K. Whitney store is built on the foundation of what was once Sidney Rigdon's tannery. Though he never used it as his residence, Sidney Rigdon was given stewardship over the tannery under the United Order in 1834 (D&C 104:20). The home is owned by the L.D.S. Church and is used for housing and not available for tours.

- **Newel K. Whitney & Co. Store** – In 1988, President Ronald Reagan awarded the President's Historic Preservation Award to the Church for its authentic restoration of the store. Drawing on Brother Whitney's meticulous records, every effort has been made to stock the shelves with items that would have been sold in the store during the 1830s. There are several things to notice in the main room that served as a store, post office, and social gathering place. Notice the uniquely designed tin lanterns hanging above your head. At night, people could recognize someone from afar by the personalized pattern of light emitted from the lantern he carried. Look closely at the shoes and boots sitting on the shelves and you will notice that there is no right or left foot. Though uncomfortable by today's standard, the shoes could be worn on either foot for longer and more even wear. Also notice the straw and silk bonnets. The peach lining of the hat helped highlight a woman's skin, giving her a "peaches and cream" complexion. The southeast room served as the work and trade room as well as the Bishop's Storehouse. Bartering was a common practice in those days and goods brought in for trade were stored here. Here too was the beginning of our modern day welfare system. In those days, the Saints would hold fast and testimony meeting on the first Thursday of each month. Items donated from their fast were received at the store and in turn given out to those

Newel K. Whitney Store

in need. The Prophet and his young family lived here for about 18 months from 1832 to 1834. In the kitchen, you can almost imagine Joseph, Emma, their surviving adopted twin daughter, and their tiny son, Joseph III, seated at the table. Notice the swingout fireplace crane holding the kettle. This extended arm helped Emma keep her long dress away from the flames of the fire. Infections resulting from serious burns were the second leading cause of death for women in those days. Also notice the herbs drying above the fireplace. This was a convenient location when the dinner meal needed a "pinch" of spice. Also of interest is the courting lantern on the mantle. When the wick burned out, the young man knew it was time to go home (more favored suitors were given longer wicks). Going upstairs, the northwest room was Joseph and Emma's bedroom. On the original tulip wood floor you can still see some of the original buttermilk paint (pigment mixed with buttermilk).

Joseph Smith's Office

Joseph III was born in this room. He later became president of the RLDS Church (now Community of Christ). Also, upstairs are two very significant rooms. The northeast room housed the School of the Prophets from January to April of 1833. Remarkable spiritual manifestations, doctrinal discussions, and revelations were received in this room. Joseph used the southeast corner room to run the affairs of the Church. The table in this room is believed to be the Prophet's original table. Here too, the Prophet received the revelation known as the Word of Wisdom (D&C 89). Joseph also worked here on the inspired revision of the Bible. The many revelations Joseph received in the Whitney store are found in D&C 84-98, 101, and possibly 78.

- **Whitney & Gilbert Livery Stable Site** – Across the street from the Whitney Store is a sign indicating the former site of the Whitney & Gilbert livery stable. From 1829 to 1831, Newel K. Whitney and his friend and business partner Algernon Sidney Gilbert had a livery stable located here. Newel and Sidney both joined the

Church in the winter of 1830. In June of 1831, Sidney journeyed with the Prophet Joseph to Independence (D&C 53). There he established a store as commanded in D&C 57:8. In the fall of 1833, mobs ransacked Brother Gilbert's store and he and his family were driven from Jackson County, as were the other Saints. Sidney and his family relocated near Rush Creek, just east of Liberty. In June of 1834, five members of Zion's Camp who were stricken with cholera died at Brother Gilbert's home. On June 29, Brother Gilbert also passed away from this same disease (HC 2:18). His name is listed on the Zion's Camp Memorial located in Independence, Missouri.

- **Newel K. Whitney Home** – The home of Newel and Elizabeth Ann Whitney has been restored to its original condition both inside and out. After arriving from New York, Emma and Joseph lived here with the Whitney family for a few weeks (HC 1:145). During their stay, Joseph healed Elsa Johnson's arm, resulting in several conversions, and the Prophet received a revelation that Edward Partridge should be the first bishop of the Church (D&C 41:11). Other revelations received here are recorded in D&C 42–44. It is also likely that Joseph received D&C 70 and 72 here.

Whitney Home

- **Whitney Red Store Site** – Just to the right of the Whitney home is a sign indicating the former site of the Whitney Red Store. In the early 1820s, Newel K. Whitney built a store here. The building also included living quarters for his family. By 1827, Brother Whitney had moved his business across the street into the larger store and had also relocated his family to a new home. Following their move, Newel's business partner Algernon Sidney Gilbert and his family probably lived here from 1827 until 1831.

- **John Johnson Inn** – This was the first brick building in Kirtland. Originally built by Peter French as an inn, it was ideally located on a small piece of land at the intersection of Chillicothe and Kirtland-Chardon Roads. The Church purchased the inn from Peter in 1833 and John Johnson was later given stewardship of the building under the Kirtland United Order (D&C 104:34). After the printing press in Independence, Missouri was destroyed, a temporary printing office was set up here which produced the *Evening & Morning Star*. The Prophet recorded that ancient Egyptian mummies and records were exhibited here (HC 2:396). Joseph had purchased the four mummies and two rolls of papyrus from Michael Chandler in 1835. On May 4, 1835, the Twelve Apostles departed from the Johnson Inn on their first mission (HC 2:219). The reconstructed inn, located on the original foundation, now features a small theater, exhibits on the legacy of

John Johnson Inn

Kirtland, a topographical model of Kirtland in the 1830s, and a hands-on computer station where visitors can check for ancestors who once lived here. Both the Whitney home and the Johnson Inn are part of the walking tour taken from the visitors' center.

- **Warren Parrish Home** – The red home located just north of the Whitney Store once belonged to Warren Parrish. Warren was a member of Zion's Camp, went on several missions, served as clerk and scribe for Joseph, and was very involved with the Kirtland Safety Society. Warren was accused of embezzling $25,000 from the Kirtland Safety Society and he eventually left the Church. He and Wilford Woodruff

Warren Parrish Home

were once missionary companions. Wilford lived in this home for a time both before his marriage to Phoebe Carter and again after their marriage. The home is owned by the Church and used for housing. It is not available for tours.

- **John F. Boynton Home** – This small home once belonged to John Boynton, one of the original Twelve Apostles. Though John eventually left the Church, he

John Boynton Home

later visited Brigham Young in Utah. The home is located just north of the Parrish home. It is owned by the Church but used for housing and is not available for tours.

- **Isaac Morley Farm** – This former 260-acre farm was the home of a religious group led by Isaac Morley called "The Family." After Isaac's baptism in 1830, many of the early arriving Saints temporarily lived on his farm. Joseph and Emma lived here with the Morleys from March thru September of 1831 before moving to Hiram. Many significant events occurred at this farm during their six-month stay. On April 30, Emma gave birth to twins, Thaddeus and Louisa, who died three hours later. Nine days later, Joseph and Emma received and adopted the Murdock twins, Joseph and Julia, whose mother had died while giving birth (HC 1:260). The fourth conference of the Church was held at the Morley farm from June 3 to June 6. At least one session took place in a small log schoolhouse located atop the hill. During this meeting, the Prophet Joseph "saw the heavens open and Jesus Christ sitting on the right hand of the Father" (CHFT p. 100). The first high priests in this dispensation were called and ordained at this conference (HC 1:175-176). Three years later, in 1834, Joseph prophesied in this schoolhouse that the Church would fill the world and that the Saints would go to the Rocky Mountains. Revelations Joseph received here are recorded in D&C 45–50, 52-56, 63 and 64. Joseph worked on the inspired translation of the Bible while living on the farm. Isaac Morley and his wife, Lucy, remained faithful to the end. They followed the Prophet to Far West and then to Nauvoo. Lucy died from typhoid fever in 1847 while living in Winter Quarters, after the Saints' expulsion from Nauvoo. Isaac led a company west to the Salt Lake Valley.

First settling in Bountiful, he later moved to southern Utah. He died at the age of 79 in 1865, and is buried in Manti, Utah. Though Lucy and Isaac's home and the log schoolhouse are no longer standing, don't miss the missionary guided tour of this special area. Tours at the Morley farm are given May thru October, from Monday thru Saturday 9 a.m.– 6 p.m. and Sunday noon – 7 p.m. Picnic tables and restrooms are located here. To visit the farm, turn left as you leave the LDS visitors' center onto Kirkland/Chardon Road. Turn right onto Chillicothe Road (Route 615). The farm will be on your left, just one mile from the visitors' center, at 8605 Chillicothe Road. 440-256-2694.

- **Kirtland Temple** – The temple is owned by the Community of Christ (formerly RLDS). Tours of the Kirtland Temple begin next door at their visitors' center. Allow one hour to view a brief video and take a tour of the temple. As you enter the Kirtland Temple, notice the original railing on the left side of the foyer, the large arched window that provides light for the first two floors, and the dangling rope which travels up through four trap doors until it reaches the bell tower located atop the temple. In the assembly rooms located on the first two floors, notice the choir lofts, the four-tiered Melchizedek Priesthood pulpits located on the west end, and the Aaronic Priesthood pulpits on the east end. The bottom tiered pulpits have

°Courtesy of Community of Christ

Melchizedek Priesthood Pulpits

a drop-leaf table which was used for the sacrament. Rollers in the ceilings held curtains which could divide the rooms into four sections (although the curtains were never installed on the second floor). The benches in the assembly rooms could be moved to allow seating in either direction. The five rooms located on the third floor were used for offices, ordinances, and schooling for the early Saints. Joseph used the far west room, also known as The President's Room, as his office. Many significant events took place in this room including: translation work, the teaching of Hebrew, and the receipt of several revelations including the vision now recorded in D&C 137 concerning the doctrine of salvation. In this revelation, the Prophet saw his beloved deceased brother, Alvin, in the celestial kingdom. (Read about this sacred experience in HC 2:379-382.) Inside the visitors' center, notice part of the original temple weathervane, a portion of the original stucco, as well as other artifacts and pictures from the 1830s. Items you may wish to purchase include copies of the Kirtland Bank Notes ($2), a copy of the original hymnal that Emma compiled ($16.95), maps, small souvenir items, tin ware,

°Courtesy of Community of Christ

Assembly Room

reprints of selected items, photos, and several books about early Kirtland (including this book). The Kirtland Temple is open March thru October, Monday thru Saturday 9 a.m.–5 p.m. and Sunday 1 p.m.–5 p.m. In November & December, open Monday thru Saturday 10 a.m.–4 p.m. and Sunday 1 p.m.–4 p.m. Open on weekends only in January & February (same weekend hours as in November & December). Closed on major holidays. There is a $2/ per person preservation fee to take the guided tour of the Kirtland Temple. The temple is located one mile south of I-90 at 9020 Chillicothe Road (Route 306). 440-256-3318.

- **Printing Office/Schoolhouse Site** – Just behind or west of the temple (now part of the parking lot), stood a two-story building. The first floor was used as a schoolhouse and the top floor served as an office for the First Presidency, a meetinghouse, and a printing office. After the building was dedicated in 1834, the School of the Prophets and Elders was moved here from the Whitney Store (HC 2:169-171). The men worked on religious studies and also on grammar and penmanship. During a conference held here, the Twelve Apostles were called and ordained (HC 2:180-200). Joseph also received D&C 134, and probably D&C 107 here. After the press was destroyed in Independence, a new press, brought by Oliver Cowdery, was used to print the first edition of the Doctrine and Covenants (which included "Lectures on Faith"), the second edition of the Book of Mormon, the Evening and Morning Star newspaper, and the hymnal Emma was told to compile in D&C 25. The building was destroyed by fire in January of 1838.

- **Kirtland Safety Society Bank Site** – The Safety Society building once stood south of the temple, where the circular walkway is presently located. On January 2, 1837, the Kirtland Safety Society was organized with Sidney Rigdon serving as chairman and Warren Parrish as secretary (HC 2:470). But soon after the first notes were issued, the business began to struggle, and ultimately had to close in November of that same year. Its failure can be attributed to several things including: a nationwide panic in May of 1837 which brought the collapse of many other banks, efforts by enemies of the Church to destroy confidence in the business, and some individual acts of dishonesty. Though the Prophet supported the Safety Society at first, business decisions were made against his advice and some Church members chose not to follow his counsel (HC 2:487). The collapse of the Kirtland Safety Society fueled the anger of some of the Saints. They "spoke against the Prophet and accused him of being responsible for all of their problems" (CHFT p. 173). Persecution of the Prophet escalated to the point that Joseph was no longer safe in Kirtland (HC 3:1). (For additional information, see "Kirtland Economy" in *Encyclopedia of Mormonism*.)

- **North Kirtland Cemetery** – Many notable Saints are buried in the small cemetery located directly north of the Kirtland Temple. Hyrum's first wife, Jerusha Smith, died in 1837 just 11 days after giving birth to their sixth child (HC 2:519). Hyrum was in Far West, Missouri at the time of her death. Also buried here is Mary Duty Smith, Joseph's paternal grandmother. Mary and her husband Asael Smith were living in Tunbridge, Vermont at the time their son, Joseph Sr., met his future wife. In May 1836, Mary, then widowed and 93 years old, made the difficult trip to Kirtland for a joyful reunion with her extended family, but died just ten days after her arrival on May 27, 1836 (HC 2:443). Though the exact location of their graves is not known, a marker located in the middle of the cemetery honors these women. Others buried here include John Johnson, Oliver Granger (read D&C 117:12), and William Cowdery (Oliver's father). Joseph

and Emma's twins (Louisa and Thaddeus) and Parley Pratt's first wife (Thankful Halsey Pratt) are also probably buried here, though the exact locations are unknown. You can read about a blessing Thankful received, promising the birth of a son, and about her death in *Autobiography of Parley P. Pratt* pages 130, 166-167.

- **Joseph Smith Home** – Joseph and Emma moved from the Newel K. Whitney Store into this home in February 1834. The Prophet received revelations here that are recorded in D&C 102, 103, and 108 and possibly 104 and 106. Joseph received many visitors in this home and also conducted Church business (possibly the organizing of Zion's Camp). Here too, the Egyptian mummies and papyri were displayed and translation began on the Book of Abraham. For a brief time, Joseph also had a variety store located across the street. It is quite likely that his son, Frederick G. Williams Smith, was born here on June 20, 1836. Less than two years later, the Prophet received a revelation (unpublished) on January 12, 1838, telling Joseph and

Joseph Smith Home

Sidney Rigdon to flee for their safety (HC 3:1). They left that night and their families joined them a few days later. Emma was expecting a child at the time, making the long and arduous journey to Far West, Missouri even more difficult. The home is located at 8980 Chillicothe Road (front and possibly middle section of the home are original). It is owned by the Community of Christ and is not available for tours.

- **Sidney Rigdon Home** – Sidney's home (greatly remodeled) is located across the street and just south from the Kirtland Temple. Sidney was a prominent minister in nearby Mentor when he was introduced to the gospel by Oliver Cowdery, Parley P. Pratt, and the other missionaries traveling from New York to teach the Lamanites (D&C 28:8). Sidney was baptized in 1830, as were many of those in his congregation. He later served as Joseph Smith's first counselor. The home is owned by the Community of Christ and is not available for tours.

Sidney Rigdon Home

- **Hyrum Smith Home** – The Prophet's beloved older brother was one of the Eight Witnesses of the Book of Mormon. He was a member of Zion's Camp, and served as a counselor in the First Presidency. While living in Nauvoo, Hyrum was called as patriarch to the Church and told to "bear record of the things which I shall show unto him" (D&C 124:96). The home is located south of the Kirtland Temple and across the street from a Sunoco gas station at 9097 Chillicothe Road. (The newer front part of the home stands on the original foundation while the back part of the home is the original.) The home is owned

Hyrum Smith Home

by the LDS Church and is currently used as housing for missionaries and not available for tours.

- **John Johnson Home** – John Johnson and his family moved into this home after moving from their farm in nearby Hiram. Here in 1835, the Prophet performed the marriage of John F. Boynton (then serving as an apostle) and his bride. John Johnson and his wife were very supportive of Joseph and the Church. For a time, Joseph and Emma lived with the Johnson family on their Hiram

John Johnson Home

farm. John's generous monetary contributions allowed the Church to purchase a great deal of land (including the Kirtland Temple property). Unfortunately, John and his son, Lyman, ultimately left the Church. The home is located southwest of the North Kirtland Cemetery at 7762 Maple Street. It is privately owned and not available for tours.

- **William Miller Home** – William was baptized at Kirtland in 1834. He followed the Prophet from Kirtland to Missouri, and then on to Nauvoo. Brother Miller once left the Nauvoo Temple dressed as Brigham Young and was arrested by the waiting marshals. After arriving in Carthage, they eventually discovered they had captured a "bogus Brigham." While living in Winter Quarters during the winter of 1846, Brother Miller and his family lived in a dugout. After their arrival in Utah, William played an active part in the settlements of both Provo and Springville. He served a mission to England, was a probate judge in Utah County, and later served as president of the Utah Stake (serving as a bishop in Provo at the same time). William Miller died in 1875 in Provo, Utah. His home (greatly remodeled) is located at 7799 Joseph Street (2nd home on your right). It is owned by the Community of Christ and is not available for tours.

- **Vinson Knight & William Marks Home** – This home was owned (at different times) by both William Marks and Vinson Knight. William Marks was baptized in New York in 1835. He once served as president of the Kirtland Stake and later in the same position in the Nauvoo Stake. He left the Church and later assisted in starting the RLDS Church (now Community of Christ), serving as a counselor to Joseph Smith III. Vinson Knight served as a counselor in a bishopric in Kirtland, and was called as acting bishop in Adam-ondi-Ahman (until the arrival of Bishop Newel K. Whitney). Brother Knight died at Nauvoo in 1842. The home is located on the northwest corner at 7741 Joseph Street. (Joseph Street is located almost directly across the road from the Hyrum Smith home.) The home is owned by the Community of Christ and is not available for tours.

- **Temple Stone Quarry** – This area was once known as the Stannard Stone Quarry. It is still possible to see the old drill marks in what is now called the Chapin Forest Reserve Park. To quarry the stone, workmen drilled a series  of holes in the sandstone, placed a wedge in each hole, and split the stone by striking the wedge with a hammer. On June 5, 1833, the Prophet's cousin, George A. Smith, hauled the first load of stone from the quarry and Hyrum Smith and Reynolds Cahoon began digging trenches for the temple walls (HC 1:353). The park includes picnic tables, hiking trails, and a small pond and makes a great recreational stop for families. Admission is free and it is open daily from sunrise to sunset. To find the quarry, head south on Chillicothe Road (also known as Route 306); the entrance will be about 2 miles from the temple on your right. Turn right after entering and park. The gravel path to your right will lead you to a wooden walkway along the old quarry.

- **Fairport Harbor Lakefront Park** – This is both a Church historical site and a fun recreational stop. Located about 13 miles northeast of Kirtland, Fairport Harbor was an important port for early Church members. Many of the Saints coming from New York traveled by flatboat on the Erie Canal to Buffalo, continued by ship to Fairport, and then rode/walked the 13 miles from the harbor to Kirtland. Arriving Saints included Lucy Mack Smith with her children (HJS p. 271), the Colesville Saints, and Joseph's paternal grandmother – Mary Duty Smith (HC 2:442). Those departing on missions also used this port. In 1835, the Twelve Apostles sailed from Fairport on a mission to the eastern states (HC 2:222). Heber C. Kimball, Orson Hyde, and others also left from this port en route to their missions to England in 1837 (HC 2:493). The park is open year round from dawn to dusk. Admission: $3/car. The park includes a beach with lifeguard on duty from Memorial Day thru Labor Day, a picnic area w/barbeque grills, playground, concession stands and restrooms. Overlooking the lake is a lighthouse with 76 steps up to the top for a great view (rebuilt and not the original lighthouse which greeted early Saints to Kirtland). At the base of the lighthouse, notice the marker placed by the Mormon Historic Sites Foundation. Attached to the lighthouse is a maritime museum, open from Memorial Day thru Labor Day on Wed., Sat., and Sunday 1 p.m.–6 p.m. Admission: adults/$3 and

children/$1. Located at 301 Huntington Beach Drive. Take 306 N. to Hwy 2 and go east to the Fairport Harbor/ Richmond Road exit. After exiting, head north until the road makes a "Y"; stay to the right going up the small rise. Turn left on Second Street and follow the signs. The lighthouse/entrance to the harbor is on your right. 440-639-9972 or www.lakevisit.com

THINGS TO DO

- **"This is Kirtland!"** – This hour-long live production explains the role of the Church in Ohio's history through a musical/theatrical format. In 2010, performances are scheduled July 2, 3, 8-10 and 15-17. The program begins at 7:30 p.m. in the Kirtland Stake Center at 8751 Kirtland Road. Admission is free but seating is limited. For groups of 20 or more, for the 2009 schedule, or for questions, contact the Kirtland visitors' center or visit www.thisiskirtland.org.

- **Penitentiary Glen** – For those with children, I would almost consider this a "must do." The 422-acre park includes a nature center, wildlife reserve, butterfly garden, hiking trails (some stroller-friendly) including a 1-mile path to see the gorge, and picnic areas. Children and adults alike will enjoy the hands-on nature center located in the main building. It is very kid-friendly with interesting exhibits, activity centers, and even includes a working beehive. Hop aboard one of the miniature steam engine trains for a free ride through the woodlands and along the rim of the gorge (check at nature center for current schedule). Entrance to the nature center is free and open daily 9 a.m.–5 p.m. The park is also open daily from sunrise to sunset. Admission is free. Located at 8668 Kirtland-Chardon Road. (Turn right as you leave the LDS visitors' center and go about 2 miles.) 440-639-7275.

- **The Holden Arboretum** – Features 3,100 acres of gardens, ponds, natural woodlands, and horticultural collections. Numerous trails offer a variety of breathtaking options. Admission: adults/$6, seniors/$5 (but free on Tuesdays), children/$3 (under 5 are free). Open daily 9 a.m.–5 p.m. Located at 9500 Sperry Road. (Continue past Penitentiary Glen and watch for the signs.) For more information or to see about tram tours (available April thru Oct.). www. holdenarb.org or 440-946-4400.

- **James A. Garfield National Historic Site** – Learn more about the 20th President of the United States, James A. Garfield, and see his home as it looked in the 1880s. Once referred to as "Lawnfield" because of the expansive grounds, the 8 acre site also includes a visitors' center and museum store. Admission is $5/adults. Open Monday thru Saturday 10 a.m.–5 p.m. and Sunday noon–5 p.m. (Nov. thru April – Open Sat. & Sunday only.) Located at 8095 Mentor Avenue. 440-255-8722.

- **Ice Skating Rink** – Visit the Mentor Civic Arena for some fun on the ice. Open ice skating sessions are offered daily from October thru April and closed May thru early June. Contact the Mentor Civic Arena for summer hours. By showing this book, you will receive one free admission with the price of one paid admission. Located at 8600 Munson Road, Mentor. 440-974-5730. **D**

- **Civic Center Water Park** – Beat the heat at a nearby water park. Featuring a 165 ft. waterslide and children's interactive water play area; all fully handicap-accessible. Show this book to receive $2 off admission price of $6/adult and $5.50/children. Open 1 p.m.-9 p.m. Memorial Day thru Labor Day. Located in front of the Mentor Civic Arena at 8600 Munson Road, Mentor. 440-974-8260. **D**

- **Lake Farmpark** – Milk a cow, take a wagon ride or see baby animals at this family oriented farm. Admission: adults/$6, seniors/$5, children/$4. Open daily 9 a.m.–5 p.m. (closed Jan.–March). Located at 8800 Chardon Road, Kirtland. 440-256-2122 or 1-800-366-3276.

- **Mentor Headlands State Park** – Enjoy a mile-long natural sand beach on Lake Erie. The park includes a playground, picnic pavilion, bbq area, restrooms, and concession stand. Lifeguard on duty from Memorial Day thru Labor Day. Open 8 a.m. to sunset year round. Located next to Mentor Lagoons Nature Preserve at State Route 44 and Headlands Road. Take 615 North to Route 2 East and exit at Route 44 North. Turn left after exiting to reach the beach entrance.

- **Cedar Point Amusement Park** – Rated as one of the best and most exciting parks and often referred to as the roller coaster capitol of the world, Cedar Point features 68 rides including 16 roller coasters! Located west of Cleveland in Sandusky, Ohio. For more information and to purchase tickets on-line (saves waiting in long lines), visit www.cedarpoint.com

- **Geauga Lake and Wildwater Kingdom** – Located about 30 miles south of Kirtland just off Route 306. (See Hiram chapter – Things to do.)

- **Visit an Amish Community** – (See Hiram chapter – Things to do.)

- **Pro Football Hall of Fame** – Located one-hour south of Cleveland at 2121 George Halas Dr., next to Fawcett Stadium in Canton, Ohio. Open daily except Christmas. Call 330-456-8207 or 800-533-4302 for more information.

- Things of interest in nearby **Cleveland** include the Cleveland Metroparks Zoo, the Cleveland Museum of Natural History, the Cleveland Museum of Art, the Cleveland Browns Stadium, and the Rock and Roll Hall of Fame. For more information, contact the Cleveland Tourism Department at 800-321-1001.

PHOTO SPOTS

- **LDS Historical Sites** – Exterior/interior pictures are allowed at all of the Church sites.

- Though there are many wonderful spots to stand and take pictures of the exterior façade of the Kirtland Temple, interior picture taking is not allowed.

- Be sure to take photos at Penitentiary Glen, the quarry, and Fairport Harbor. You can't help but be inspired by the beauty of nature.

LDS CHURCH SERVICES

Sacrament Meeting begins at 9 a.m. in the Kirtland Ward. The chapel is located at 8751 Kirtland Road. (This building was rebuilt in 1987 after an arsonist burned the previous one in 1986.) Check at www.lds.org to verify current meeting times.

ATM

You will find an ATM at the Great Lakes Mall, at Charter One Bank at 8715 (Mentor), Key Bank on Plaza Blvd., and at many other local banks.

SHOPPING

- **Great Lakes Mall** – Featuring over 140 stores including Dillard's, J.C. Penney's, Kaufmann's, and Sears. Located at 7850 Mentor Avenue.

- **Wal-Mart** – Located at 9303 Mentor Avenue (close to the Boston Market restaurant). 440-974-3300.

RESTAURANTS

- **RJ's** – Locally owned family-friendly restaurant (casual and non-smoking). Choices include pasta, pizza, sandwiches, and barbeque dinners. Call ahead to order box lunches. Group catering also available. Open daily from 11 a.m.–10 p.m., Monday thru Thursday (closes at 8 p.m. on Sunday and 11 p.m. on Friday and Saturday). Located three blocks south of the Kirtland Temple at 9264 Chillicothe Road, Willoughby. 440-256-4757. **D**

- **Subway** – Located next to RJ's. 440-256-7827.

You will also find a large selection of restaurants in two separate areas: on 306 (heading north from the LDS visitors' center) and on Mentor Avenue.

Located on Route 306 (after leaving the visitors' center):

- **Choices include:** McDonald's, Long John Silver's, Ponderosa, T.G.I. Friday's, Cookers, Red Lobster, Arby's, and Bob Evans.

Located on/near Mentor Avenue:

- **Mama Roberto's** – Locally owned Italian restaurant (casual & non-smoking). Featuring pasta, pizza, veal, chicken, calzones, and more. Reasonable prices and large size portions (carry out or catering also available). Open Tuesday thru Saturday 11 a.m.–9 p.m., Sunday 3 p.m.–9 p.m., and Monday 4 p.m.–9 p.m. Located in Village Plaza at 8658 Mentor Ave. 440-205-8890. **D**

- **Panera Bread** – Both a bakery and deli, featuring homemade soups and sandwiches. Open 7 a.m.–9p.m. daily. Located on the corner of Route 306/Mentor Avenue at 7357 Mentor Ave. 440-975-9022.

- **Other choices include:** Frozen Custard, Taco Bell, Wendy's, Arby's, Denny's, Olive Garden, Papa John's, McDonald's, Dairy Queen, Subway, Applebee's, KFC, Pizza Hut, Bob Evans, and Boston Market.

- **Yours Truly** – George W. Bush dined here in 2005. Featuring breakfast menu, salads, burgers, broiled items and more. Located at 7280 Center Street, Mentor. 440-954-9393.

LODGING

The Kirtland area has many lodging choices. Most of the following are located within close proximity to the Kirtland Temple and LDS visitors' center.

- **Lawnfield Inn and Suites** – Newer, charming Victorian style hotel (smoke free) with attached historical home. Featuring 50 rooms, double and king suites. Includes fitness center, business center, and outdoor heated pool. Rates begin at $72 w/deluxe continental breakfast included. Located 1.2 miles from exit #195/Route 615 and 4 miles from Kirtland Temple at 8434 Mentor Avenue, Mentor. 866-205-7378. **D**

- **Days Inn Cleveland/Willoughby** – Days Inn is offering a 15% discount to those showing this book. Room rates begin at $59 with continental breakfast included (fridge and microwave in each room). Other features include outdoor pool, coin-operated laundry, and interior corridors with vending area. Located 1 mile from Historic Kirtland at 4145 State Route 306, Willoughby. 440-946-0500. **D**

- **Red Roof Inn** – Featuring 108 rooms with cable T.V. Rates start at $40 (reflecting a 20% discount). Pets welcome. Located next to Burger King. Conveniently located 1.3 miles from Kirtland sites at 4166 Route 306, Willoughby. 440-946-9872. **D**

- **Comfort Inn** – The Comfort Inn is offering a special year-round discounted room rate of $90 with continental breakfast included. Everyone will enjoy the indoor pool, whirlpool, and fitness room. Bus groups are welcome.

Located only 3 miles from Kirtland at 7701 Reynolds Road, Mentor. 440-951-7333. **D**

- **Courtyard By Marriott** – You can't help but enjoy your stay at the Courtyard with its 90 executive rooms and suites (each with whirlpool). Other amenities include an indoor pool, exercise room, business services, and on-site restaurant. Located about 5 miles from Historic Kirtland sites at 35103 Maplegrove Road, Willoughby (exit 189). 440-530-1100. **D**

- **Holiday Inn Express Hotel and Suites** – Enjoy 76 rooms and suites starting at $88 with deluxe continental breakfast included. Amenities include fitness center, restaurant (w/ discounted Sunday brunch), gift shop, conference center, swimming pool and coin-operated laundry. Located less than 10 miles from Kirtland at 5785 Heisley Road, Mentor. 440-357-0384. **D**

- **Hampton Inn** – Featuring 123 rooms beginning at $80 with deluxe continental breakfast included. Amenities include indoor swimming pool and exercise room. Located 13 miles from downtown Cleveland and about 15 miles from the Kirtland historic sites at 28611 Euclid Avenue, Wickliffe. 440-944-4030. **D**

- **Ramada Plaza** – Full service hotel with 213 guestrooms, many non-smoking and all with high-speed Internet access. Room rates start at $79. Amenities include elevators, indoor pool, fitness center, game room, laundry facilities, and on-site restaurants. Located 8.5 miles from historic Kirtland, just off I-90 at 28600 Ridgehills Drive, Wickliffe. 800-752-2582. **D**

- **Punderson Manor State Park Resort** – English Tudor mansion in tranquil park setting (see Hiram – camping). Situated 30 minutes from Kirtland while en route to the John Johnson Farm at 11755 Kinsman Road, Newbury. 800-282-7275 or 440-564-9144.

- **Super 8 Motel** – 64-room motel; located at 7325 Palisades Parkway, Mentor. 800-800-8000 or 440-951-8558.

- **Radisson Hotel** – Located at 3500 Curtis Blvd., Eastlake. 440-953-8000.

- **Renaissance Quail Hollow Resort** – Full-service hotel w/176 rooms and on-site restaurant. Located at 11080 Concord-Hambden Road, Concord. 800-468-3571 or 440-497-1100.

CAMPING

- **Punderson State Park/Resort** – To read about Punderson State Park and several other camping options see Hiram chapter.

Notes

Notes

Notes

Notes

Notes

_____

_____

_____

_____

_____

_____

_____

_____

_____

_____

_____

_____

_____

_____

_____

_____

_____

_____

Notes

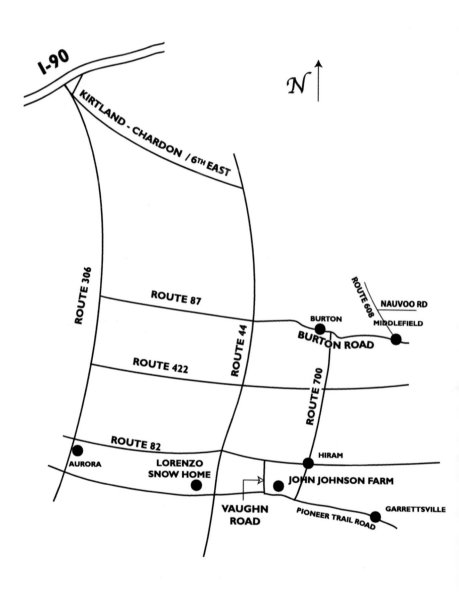

Chapter Eighteen
Hiram

Hiram Township, with a population around 2,000, lies about 32 miles southeast of Kirtland. Located here is Hiram College, established in 1850. U. S. President James A. Garfield attended this college for three years. Later, he returned as a professor and also served as president of the college. Here too, President Garfield fell in love with and later married one of his classmates, Lucretia Rudolph.

Of greater significance for L.D.S. history, Hiram was also the home of John Johnson. In 1818, John, his wife Alice (usually referred to as Elsa), and their children moved from Vermont to Hiram. First living in a log cabin, John became a prosperous farmer and built a large farm home in 1829. While active in the Methodist church, John and Elsa went to Kirtland to meet the Prophet after receiving a Book of Mormon. Elsa had such severe rheumatism that one arm was almost useless. After the Prophet miraculously healed Elsa's arm, she and John joined the Church and became good friends with Joseph, even inviting him to come live with them. (Read about this miracle in HC 1:215-216.)

From September 1831 to September 1832, the farm was not only the home of John Johnson, his wife, and their children, it was also the home of Joseph, Emma, and their newly adopted twins. John and Elsa rearranged their lives and their home to accommodate the Prophet and his family. Luke and Lyman, two of the Johnson's sons, became two of the original members of the Quorum of the Twelve Apostles. In addition, one of the Johnson's daughters, Marinda, married Orson Hyde, another member of the Quorum of the Twelve.

PLANNING YOUR TIME

Though Hiram is about 35 miles away from Kirtland, allow 2 hours for the round trip drive on country roads. The guided tour of the Johnson home is about 45 minutes. Just minutes from the Johnson farm in the town of Mantua, is the birthplace of Lorenzo Snow. Drive by the home and read a brief synopsis about the Prophet Lorenzo Snow included at the end of this chapter. Several other possible activities are mentioned if time allows.

GETTING THERE

The John Johnson farm is located almost 35 miles southeast of Kirtland. Traveling south from the Kirtland Temple on Route 306, drive about 22.5 miles before coming to the intersection of Route 306 and Route 82 (you are now near Aurora and Geauga Lake Wildwater Kingdom). Turn left on Route 82 and drive east about 7 miles. After passing the intersection of Route 82 and Route 44, continue on Route 82 for about 1.5 miles. Watch for the Johnson farm sign and turn right on Vaughn Road. Drive south about 0.5 miles on Vaughn Road until you reach Pioneer Trail Road. Turn left and head east on Pioneer Trail. The John Johnson farm is located about 1.5 miles on your left at 6203 Pioneer Trail.

You can also reach the Johnson farm by driving southeast on Kirtland-Chardon Road/6th East and turning right onto Route 44, heading south. Continue south on Route 44 and turn left onto Route 82, heading east for about 1.5 miles. Watch for the Johnson farm sign and turn right on Vaughn Road and follow the same directions given for the previous route.

The Amish area in and around Burton and Middlefield is just east of Route 44. Driving through this countryside, either on your way down to the Johnson farm or en route back to Kirtland, is about a 30-minute detour.

SIGNIFICANT EVENTS

Many sacred events occurred while the Prophet was living here: Joseph and Sidney Rigdon worked on the inspired revision of the Bible, the Prophet received 16 revelations, Joseph received a vision concerning the three degrees of glory, the publication of the Book of Commandments was approved in a conference, and the headquarters of the Church was located here. In contrast to the many spiritual happenings, a tragic event also took place; Joseph was dragged from this home, beaten, tarred and feathered by a mob. One of the twins, Joseph Murdock Smith, was sick and died a few days later as a result of exposure to the cold night air during this event.

- **Publication of the Book of Commandments approved –** On November 1, 1831, at a two-day conference held in the Johnson home, publication of the Book of Commandments was approved (later entitled D&C) (HC 1:221-225). In this conference, it was also noted that the preface to the Book of Commandments was "received by inspiration"

Revelation Room

(HC 1:222). Many are familiar with the events that would later occur on July 20, 1833, at Independence, Missouri, where the printing was started. While the printing was in process at W.W. Phelps' printing office, a mob came to destroy the press and ransack the office. Mary Elizabeth and Caroline Rollins showed great courage as they ran to gather up some of the scattered pages and then escaped from the mob by running into the nearby cornfields.

- **Joseph received a vision** – On February 16, 1832, after the Prophet had finished his translation of John 5:29, he recorded, "myself and Elder Rigdon saw the following vision ..." HC 1:245 – 253. The vision of the Father and Son and the three degrees of glory is recorded in D&C 76.

- **Inspired Revision of the Bible (Initially begun in Fayette)** – The Prophet, with Sidney Rigdon acting as scribe, worked each day on the inspired revision of the Bible. Rather than instructing Joseph to translate the Bible, the Lord had the Prophet "revise the English text of the Bible under inspiration of God; and that led him not only to give different renderings of various passages, but also to supply missing parts" (HC 1:215). Joseph worked on the revisions at the farm from November 1831 until March 1832.

- **Revelations received here** – While staying at the Johnson farm, Joseph received 16 revelations. They are recorded as D&C 1, 65, 67– 69, 71, 73, 74, 76–81, 99, and 133. The Lord's preface to the Book of Commandments (Doctrine and Covenants) is found in Section 1, while many of the other sections include instruction concerning the inspired revision of the Bible.

- **Headquarters for the Church** – The Prophet directed and conducted Church business during his stay at the Johnson home. Originally moving into the home in September 1831, Joseph went to Missouri to visit the Saints in April, but returned here to live until September 1832.

- **Joseph was beaten, tarred, and feathered** – On Saturday evening March 24, 1832, a mob of about 50 men attacked the Prophet while he lay sleeping. Joseph and Emma's adopted twins, Joseph and Julia, had been sick with the measles and Joseph had suggested that evening that Emma get some rest and he would stay up with one of the twins. As the Prophet lay sleeping on the trundle bed, the mob burst into the room and proceeded to drag him outside. After deciding not to kill him as originally planned, the mob scratched and beat the Prophet and then tarred and feathered him. They even tried to force a vial of poison in his mouth but only succeeded in breaking a piece of Joseph's tooth, which left him with a permanent slight whistle in his speech. Sidney Rigdon was also taken from his home. Dragged by his heels across the frozen ground, he suffered a severe head injury which left him delirious for several days. When Joseph regained his strength and returned to the farm, Emma saw

Joseph and Emma's Bedroom

the tar and thinking it was blood, fainted. For the rest of the night, friends helped in the painful process of scraping the tar off. Despite the attack, Joseph arose that next morning (Sunday) and, "with my flesh all scarified and defaced, I preached to the congregation as usual, and in the afternoon of the same day baptized three individuals" (HC 1:264). (Several members of the mob were among those in attendance.) The Smith's infant son Joseph, already weakened from the measles, was exposed to the cold night air and died five days later on Friday, March 29, 1832. He would have been eleven months old on the following day. (Read the Prophet's account of this attack in HC 1:261-265).

SITES TO SEE

*   **John Johnson Farm House** – On October 28, 2001, President Hinckley rededicated this special site. The home was built in 1829, purchased by the Church in 1956, and then beautifully restored with furnishings from the original period. While looking at this home, you can almost imagine the Prophet Joseph Smith as he stood on the front porch each Sunday to give a sermon. In the main kitchen, notice the original paint inside the warming cupboard and the original brick fireplace. There were five additional fireplaces in the home. The dining room, located to the right of the front door, was changed into a parlor for Joseph and Emma when they came here to live. The room just to the left of the front door was originally a parlor for the Johnson family but became Joseph and Emma's bedroom. Notice the colorful floor and the built in china closet. On March 24, 1832, Joseph was taken from this room to be beaten, tarred, and feathered. Upstairs, the top left side of the home was originally one large

John Johnson Home

room, but after the Prophet arrived, it was divided into two bedrooms, that of John and Elsa and that of their daughters. The boys likely slept in the loft. The upstairs room, on the right side, was originally the bedroom of John and Elsa, but became Joseph's study and the headquarters of the Church (and is often referred to as the Revelation Room). For a time, Joseph and Sidney worked here daily on the inspired revision of the Bible. The Prophet also received many revelations in this room. While working on John 5:29, Joseph received the revelation recorded in D&C 76 concerning the three degrees of glory. Be sure to pick up a bookmark before or after your tour concerning the revelations received here. The farm is located at 6203 Pioneer Trail Road. There is plenty of parking (east side of the home), restrooms, picnic tables, and a grassy area for children to get their wiggles out. Open Monday thru Saturday 9 a.m.–7 p.m. and Sunday 11:30 a.m.–7 p.m. Tours end at 5 p.m. during the winter. Admission is free. The farm is located at 6203 Pioneer Trail. 330-569-3374.

MANTUA

The birthplace of Lorenzo Snow is located less than 4 miles from the John Johnson farm in the town of Mantua. A brief synopsis of President Snow's life is included at the end of the chapter. It is always a great opportunity to learn more about one of our latter-day prophets at their birthplace.

GETTING THERE

Turn right as you leave the John Johnson Farm onto Pioneer Trail Road. After crossing Route 44, continue on Pioneer Trail to the next stop sign (about 4.4 miles from farm). Turn right at this stop sign onto Mantua Center Road. The framed home, set sideways to the road, will be almost immediately on your right (about .1 mile after turning). You will also notice a small cemetery near the corner.

SITES TO SEE

- **Lorenzo Snow's Birthplace** – This was once the home of Oliver and Rosetta Snow, parents of seven children including Eliza R. and Lorenzo. The Prophet Joseph Smith visited this home in the winter of 1831. As Eliza quietly watched the Prophet warming himself by the fire, she decided, "His was an honest face" (BYU Studies 11, no. 4:127). The home is located at 1118 Mantua Center Road. It is privately owned and not available for tours. Please be careful if you stop to take a picture. Mantua Center is a small country road used by many large gravel trucks.

Lorenzo Snow Home

LDS CHURCH SERVICES

The Hiram Ward Chapel is located next to the John Johnson farm at 6149 Pioneer Trail. Church meetings begin at 10 a.m. Check the Church web site at www.lds.org for current information.

ATM

An ATM is located at the Middlefield Bank on Route 82 in Garretsville (in center of town). Other locations include the Aurora Outlet Mall, Metropolitan Bank at 95 Chillicothe Road, and Bank One at 250 Garfield Road.

AMISH COMMUNITY

The area in and around Middlefield, with a current population of over 4,000, is one of the largest Amish settlements in the United States. Be careful while driving through this scenic countryside as you may suddenly come upon a slow moving horse-drawn buggy. Suggested places to stop include:

- **Mary Yoder's Amish Kitchen** – Popular Amish restaurant well known for their family style dishes including fried chicken, roast beef, soups, sandwiches, Amish date pudding, and large selection of pies. Notice the quilts adorning the walls. A bakery and gift shop are also located here. Open Monday thru Saturday. Located at 14743 North State Street (Route 608), Middlefield. 440-632-1939.

- **Middlefield Cheese** – Make a quick stop at the Middlefield Swiss Cheese factory which currently makes over 25 million pounds of cheese each year. Displays will introduce you to the art of cheese making and the gift store entices you to take some home. Open Monday thru Saturday 8 a.m.-5 p.m. Located at 15815 Nauvoo Road, Middlefield (1 mile north of Middlefield on Route 608). 440-632-5228.

- There are several Amish gift stores near the Middlefield Cheese Factory. Many of the stores have signs along the road indicating their location.

ACTIVITIES/SHOPPING

For a free tourism packet, contact the Aurora Chamber of Commerce at 330-562-3355. (Aurora is located just a few miles directly west of Hiram on Route 82.)

- **Geauga Lake and Wildwater Kingdom** – 1060 North Aurora Road, Aurora. 330-562-8303.

- **Aurora Outlet Shopping Mall** – Store selections include Nautica, Tommy Hilfiger, Gap, Brooks Brothers, etc. Located at 549 S. Chillicothe Road. 330-562-2000.

- **Camp Hi Canoe Livery** – Enjoy a 1 to 6 hour canoe or kayak trip on the Upper Cuyahoga River. 330-569-7621

- **Nelson-Kennedy Ledges State Park** – A small state park popular for hiking, picnicking, and nature sightseeing. Complete with spectacular rock formations, a beech-maple forest, and diverse plant life. Located just off Route 282 (near Punderson State Park).

- **Sugarbush Golf Course** – Located in Garrettsville (2 miles SE from Hiram). 330-527-4202

RESTAURANTS

- **Zeppe's Pizza** – Garrettsville

- Many fast foods are located in Garrettsville including McDonald's and Subway.

- **Pastimes** - Mantua

CAMPING

- **Punderson State Park/Resort** – Enjoy nature at its finest. Featuring 200 RV/camping sites ranging from $23-

$32/night with same-day reservations accepted. (For busy summer weekends, it would be wise to make a Thursday reservation to guarantee weekend availability.) Amenities include a lodge with on-site restaurant, swimming pool, lake, 18-hole golf course, hiking trails, and other nearby recreational sites. Punderson State Park is located about 30 minutes southeast of Kirtland (follow 306 south about 23 miles and go east on 87). 866-644-6727 or 440-564-1195.

- **Yogi Bear Jellystone Park Camp/Resorts** – Geared for fun family camping next to a 500-acre lake with canoes, 4 playground areas, game room, heated swimming pool, and more. Located at 3392 State Route 82, Mantua. 800-344-9644.

- **Woodside Lake Park** – 330-626-4251

- **Kool Lakes Family RV Park** – 440-548-8436

LORENZO SNOW

Lorenzo Snow, fifth President of the Church was born on April 3, 1814 in Mantua, Ohio. He was the first son and the fifth of seven children born to Oliver and Rosetta Pettibone Snow. Lorenzo's parents were leaders in the community and the Snow family was well known for their honesty. Raised as Baptists, the children read the Bible, had family prayer, and were encouraged to be broad-minded and courteous to all they met.

Lorenzo Snow

Oliver's public duties often took him away from home and Lorenzo had much of the responsibility of taking care of the farm, with the help of his two younger brothers. Because of his many chores, he often was only able to attend school during the three winter months of the year. His parents were both well educated and encouraged their children to value an education. Lorenzo especially loved to read and he spent much of his free time with a book.

When Lorenzo was very young, he learned the power of prayer. Once when he was out in the fields, a huge bull chased him up in a tree. He became cold and frightened sitting in the tree as the bull pawed at the ground below him. With his teeth chattering from the wind, he prayed that his father would come and rescue him. Just then his father came riding up on a horse and cracking his whip, scared the bull away and helped a cold Lorenzo down from the tree.

Lorenzo was especially close to his sister Eliza R. Snow, who often did nice things for him. As a young boy, he decided that he wanted to be a soldier when he grew up and Eliza made a military uniform for him. He felt he could talk to her about anything and the two remained close all of their lives.

The first time that Lorenzo Snow saw Joseph Smith was in 1831, when Lorenzo was seventeen years old. At that time, the Prophet was living in Hiram at the John Johnson farm. Lorenzo had already heard stories about Joseph and he was curious enough to want to listen to and see this man for himself. As the Prophet stood and talked at the front door of the Johnson farmhouse, Lorenzo was one of over two hundred who listened. Lorenzo would later recall that at age 25, Joseph was not yet a fluent speaker, but as he bore his testimony to the truthfulness of what he was saying, his low voice became strong and powerful. Lorenzo had a lasting impression that this was a man who was honest and sincere.

Anxious to further his education, Lorenzo sold some property he had inherited and entered nearby Oberlin College in 1835. A chance meeting with apostle David W. Patten also left a positive impression on him. While he was in Oberlin, his sister Eliza was baptized a member of the Church and taught school at the Prophet Joseph Smith's home. (His mother and sister Leonora had already joined the Church in 1831.) Eliza invited Lorenzo to come and visit her in Kirtland and study Hebrew with a professor who was teaching the leaders of the Church. His decision to go would forever change his life.

Soon after his arrival in Kirtland, Lorenzo had a chance meeting with the Prophet Joseph Smith. Again he was impressed with the feeling that this was a remarkable man. After much study and prayer, Lorenzo was baptized a member of the Church on June 19, 1836. He was 21 years old. For the rest of his life, Lorenzo remained steadfast in his convictions and anxious to serve.

Lorenzo began his many years of missionary service in the spring of 1837 as he labored in the Mantua area teaching and converting friends and relatives. He also fulfilled a mission in the Illinois and Kentucky region. From 1840 to 1843, Lorenzo served a mission in England, even presenting a copy of the Book of Mormon to Queen Victoria. Returning home with a shipload of about 250 converts, he blessed and healed a steward on the ship who was extremely ill. After landing in New Orleans, several of the officers and sailors who had witnessed the miracle were baptized.

Lorenzo was in Ohio when he learned the shocking news of the Prophet's death. At the time, he was on a different type of mission – campaigning for Joseph's candidacy for President of the United States. In 1849, at the age of 35, Lorenzo was ordained an apostle, one year after he arrived in the Salt Lake Valley. As one of his early assignments, he helped to organize the Perpetual Emigration Fund. Shortly thereafter, he was again called on a mission. From 1849 to 1852, Lorenzo spread the gospel in Europe.

Upon his return from Europe, Lorenzo was designated by Brigham Young to head the colonization of an area that is now known as Brigham City (nearby Mantua, Utah was named in honor of Lorenzo's birthplace). At age 50, he served a mission to the Hawaiian Islands. While there, Lorenzo's life was saved when his boat capsized near one of the islands. The other elders performed resuscitation on the nearly drowned Lorenzo. At age 58, he went with George A. Smith to Palestine to rededicate that land for the return of the Jews. He also served a short mission at age 71 in the northwestern states, working with the Lamanites.

Lorenzo Snow became President of the Quorum of the Twelve Apostles when he was 75 years old and president of the Salt Lake Temple at age 79. When President Wilford Woodruff became very ill and wasn't expected to live, Lorenzo went to the Salt Lake Temple to pray that President Woodruff might outlive him. But the Lord had other plans and President Woodruff passed away. Shortly after President

Woodruff's death, Lorenzo went to the Salt Lake Temple to seek guidance and instruction. While leaving the Celestial Room, he saw and talked with the Savior. On October 13, 1898, Lorenzo Snow was sustained as President of the Church at the age of 84.

President Snow was slight in stature, standing about 5 foot 6 inches and weighing less than 150 pounds. Yet he was large in gentleness, dignity, purity, and humility. When he became president, the Church was struggling financially. While speaking to a congregation in St. George, Utah, President Snow received a revelation. He told the members that they needed to become full tithe payers. He also spoke of the blessings that could be theirs and specifically promised an end to the drought they were experiencing. The members followed his counsel and as a result of their obedience to the law of tithing, the severe drought was soon replaced with heavy rains. His encouragement to all Church members to pay their tithing not only brought blessings to individuals, but also enabled the Church to get out of debt.

President Lorenzo Snow, a beloved husband, father, grandfather, and Prophet, died in the Beehive House on October 10, 1901, at the age of 87. He had served as President of the Church for 3 eventful years.

Resources to help you learn more about our latter-day prophets include *Presidents of The Church*, (Student Manual Religion 345) published by the Church and *Boys Who Became Prophets* by Lynda Cory Robison.

Notes

Notes

Notes

Notes

Notes

Discounts

The following businesses will give a one-time discount of 10% to those that present this travel guide. Exception – notice that a few businesses are offering a gift, 2 for 1, etc. instead of the 10% discount. **This discount is applicable to book owner, spouse and minor children.** Please read the corresponding chapter for more detailed information about each business and any discount exceptions.

It is the book owner's responsibility to verify price and availability of discount before purchase. Application of merchant discounts subject to change without notice. **Be sure to mention this guidebook and request the discount as you call to make lodging reservations, then present the book upon arrival to ensure discount.**

Merchants, after giving the discount, please initial on the line next to your listed business. This indicates that the one-time discount has been given.

SHARON

_____ Sugarbush Farm

_____ Baxter Mountain House B&B

_____ Comfort Suites

_____ Comfort Inn

PALMYRA

_____Historic Palmyra Museums

_____Colonial Belle

_____Latter-day Harvest Bookstore (gift)

_____Candy Corner Fudge Square

_____ Brick House Antique Center

_____Marks Pizzeria

_____Yellow Mills Diner

_____Palmyra Inn

_____Liberty House B&B

_____Quality Inn Finger Lakes Region

_____Super 8

_____Bed and Breakfast at Oliver Phelps

_____The Lodge at Woodcliff

_____Hampton Inn & Suites

_____Springdale Farm B&B

KIRTLAND

_____Civic Center Water Park ($2 off admission)

_____Ice Skating Rink (2 for 1)

_____RJ's

_____Mama Roberto's

_____Lawnfield Inn and Suites

_____Days Inn Cleveland/Willoughby (15% discount)

_____Red Roof Inn (CP 522599) (20% discount)

_____Comfort Inn (same room rate year-round)

_____Courtyard By Marriott

_____Holiday Inn Cleveland East

_____Holiday Inn Express and Suites

_____Hampton Inn

VIDEOS

In addition to the recommended list in the opening chapter, there is a commercially produced video that offers additional insight and information on this era in Church history.

- **American Prophet** – The remarkable story of the Prophet Joseph Smith, as narrated by Gregory Peck. Discusses the Prophet's life, message and influence. Available on VHS (almost two hours) for $19.95 and DVD (3 hours) for $21.95. For more information, or to place an order, visit www.grobergfilms.com. To receive a 10% discount, include the code **Nauvoo** with your on-line order.

About the Author

Becky Cardon Smith is a graduate of Brigham Young University. One of her favorite hobbies is traveling with her family. Though they have seen many of the popular sites of the world, some of the most memorable trips have been to Church historical sites. A former elementary school teacher, she can't resist the urge to search for information and dole out advice. She and her husband Greg have four children and reside in Utah.

Contact the author at www.ldsfamilytravel.com for suggestions, questions, or feedback. Please let us know if you had difficulty receiving one of the listed discounts, want to recommend a restaurant or lodging, or have a suggestion on improving the guidebook. Our goal is to make your trip to Church historical sites as wonderful and enriching as possible. Have a great trip!